SEE IT &
SINK IT

SEE IT & SINK IT

MASTERING PUTTING THROUGH PEAK VISUAL PERFORMANCE

Dr. Craig L. Farnsworth

CHAIRMAN, SPORTS EYE ENHANCEMENT

Foreword by Nick Faldo

Introduction by Dave Pelz

HarperCollins*Publishers*

SEE IT & SINK IT. Copyright © 1997 by Dr. Craig Farnsworth. All rights reserved. Printed in the United States of America. No part of this book may be used or reproduced in any manner whatsoever without written permission except in the case of brief quotations embodied in critical articles and reviews. For information address HarperCollins Publishers, Inc., 10 East 53rd Street, New York, New York 10022.

HarperCollins books may be purchased for educational, business, or sales promotional use. For information, please write to: Special Markets Department, HarperCollins Publishers, Inc., 10 East 53rd Street, New York, New York 10022.

FIRST EDITION

Designed by Irving Perkins Associates

Library of Congress Cataloging-in-Publication Data

Farnsworth, Craig L.
    See it & sink it : mastering putting through peak visual
performance / Craig L. Farnsworth. — 1st ed.
        p.   cm.
     ISBN 0-06-270203-3
     1. Putting (Golf) I. Title.
GV979.P8F37   1997
796.352'35—dc21   97-1540

97 98 99 00 01 ❖/RRD 10 9 8 7 6 5 4 3 2 1

Dedication

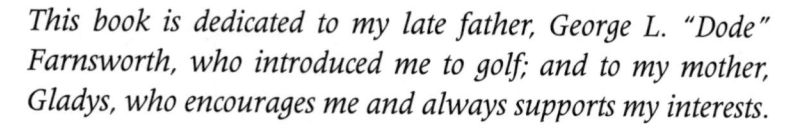

This book is dedicated to my late father, George L. "Dode" Farnsworth, who introduced me to golf; and to my mother, Gladys, who encourages me and always supports my interests.

Last, but not least, this is for all of you golfers who miss putts that you know you should make.

Contents

Acknowledgments

SPECIAL THANKS TO Clayton Cole, head golf professional at Cherry Hills Country Club in Denver. Clayton is a consummate professional who seldom misses putts he should make and gave me the perfect forum to test and expose my system to the wonderful members of Cherry Hills.

Also to my mentors, Dr. William C. Lee and Dr. William D. Harrison, thanks for your 21st century foresight. To you I am always dedicated.

And thanks to Jim and Marcia Bailey, Sue Browning, Gary Polumbus, Bob Russo, Dr. Dale Carnegie, George Brown, Bonnie and Jed Kelly, and my patient brother Brooke Farnsworth, for your insight.

To my dear wife, Mary Ann, I cannot thank you enough. My wish would be that everyone should be blessed by such a wonderful and loyal friend and confidante. And to my lovely children, Garrett and Karla, thank you for letting Dad do his thing. To Bart, thank you for getting this project into the right hands.

Last, I owe appreciation to my agent/editor, John Andrisani, who believed in this project every stretch of the way.

Foreword

IN THE PAST, I have been known for my discipline and hard work toward perfecting my swing. The irony of this game, however, is that a great swing doesn't guarantee a good score. To score, you have to sink putts.

I have always felt I had a good putting stroke. But, in 1995, I just wasn't sinking the putts that I knew I must make to continue to win. I knew something was wrong, but I didn't know what. I called Dr. Craig L. Farnsworth, an optometrist, who was doing something interesting with the eyes and perception, and had some success working with some of my colleagues.

It wasn't long into the testing phase that I knew this was something special. Dr. Farnsworth's unique tests discovered my eyes perceived the hole short and left of its actual location. When he noted that this tendency started from 15 feet out, I told him, "Amazing, that is where I start to miss regularly!"

After the testing, we moved to the practice green. I spent a good part of two days listening to Dr. Farnsworth's system and practicing his visual guidance techniques. The improvement in my putting came almost instantly. In fact, this was a contributing factor toward my win at the 1996 Masters, where I was fifth for the tournament in putting statistics.

I have enormous faith in the Farnsworth System's ability to make you a better putter. I went from 79th in

putting on the Tour in 1995 to leading the Tour for the first six months of 1996, and ending up in the top ten!

You, too, will appreciate that putting is primarily a visual challenge. How you see and what you perceive is key to putting. I am confident this book will take you to the next level on the greens.

Nick Faldo

Preface

A man who can putt is a match for anyone; a man who can't is a match for no one.

WILLIE PARK, BRITISH OPEN CHAMPION, 1887–1889

WHAT IS IT that an eye doctor like me can contribute to putting knowledge that hasn't been addressed by volumes of instructions already available? I'll tell you.

Nothing is more visual than alignment, reading the greens and judging the ball's speed for the longer putts. Recent research has found that visual misperceptions are the basis of missed putts and not faulty stroke mechanics. A disturbing fact has emerged: Most golfers misalign because they do not see what they think they see. As you will discover, the eye-brain perception of reality is easily fooled. Visual perception, if inaccurate, feeds the motor system with faulty information that results in misalignments and even a poor stroke. The good news: Perceptions can be easily altered.

You are about to learn how the Farnsworth System of putting allows you to overcome visual misperceptions and to gain the edge. In fact, mastering putting through accurate visual perceptions is what this book is all about.

The majority of pros know that the secret to low scoring is not found on the practice tee, but rather on the putting green or at home, where they utilize unique techniques to

enhance their ability to hole putts. Putting represents 40–50 percent of the strokes taken on the golf course. It does not call for strength, speed, a great deal of mechanics, or experience. But to truly lower your handicap, you must consistently make those six-foot "kneeknockers" and reduce three-putts.

You are about to experience an exciting new concept called *visual dominance*. It is based on how we see, and establish accuracy of what we perceive. This concept forms the basis of a unique technique that will elevate your scoring abilities like none other.

The Farnsworth System, and the never-before-told secrets of improving your putting through the eyes, are contained in *See It & Sink It.*

Chapter One focuses on self-tests to determine the quality of your visual perception of distance and direction, and on adaptation to the perspective of alignment in the address position.

Chapters Two and Three explore ways to better "read" greens and reduce mis-hits through visual dominance.

The Zorro and Shaft techniques contained in Chapters Four and Five will help you deal with the nemesis of alignment misperceptions, the number one problem, and the problem of visual noise.

Chapter Six discusses the difference between will and imagination, and why positive thinking may not be enough.

Chapter Seven covers visualization techniques to master the longer putts and what to do if visualization fails.

Chapter Eight conveys why the hole is seldom the target, and ways to factor uphill and downhill putts.

Chapter Nine spells out the use of a specific Game Plan.

Chapter Ten addresses The Moment Of Truth. Here, you will learn how to avoid self-distractions that interfere with your task, on and off the golf course. You will experience, too, why age-old concepts, such as "feel," need to be replaced by the visual system's interpretation of the

green's characteristics. Further, you will learn how to quiet the mind before addressing the ball, and overcome those subconscious demons that disrupt your stroke.

This book's recommendations will literally provide you with an entirely new way of *looking* at the game of golf. Enjoy *See It & Sink It* as it takes you on a journey of discovery, where old concepts do not apply and are replaced with more fundamentally sound and easily applied laws of performance. Get ready to acquire the eye of a champion via enlightening information that has changed the putting games of Nick Faldo and my other pro and amateur students.

Incidentally, as great a player as Faldo is, he realized he had problems aligning the putter, seeing the line, and visualizing the ball dropping into the hole. With the help of the Farnsworth System, he's back on track. In fact, almost all of the secrets contained in this book have been used by Nick. Have the courage to face up to your own faults, and let *See It & Sink It* be your guidebook to self-improvement on the greens.

Dr. Craig Farnsworth
Chairman
Sports Eye Enhancements, Inc.
1999 Broadway, Suite 2400
Denver, Colorado 80202

Introduction

Dear Golfer,

I have had the opportunity to work with and watch a number of great golfers. I've also seen how, in the final analysis, putting can dictate whether they win or lose.

Most golfers have observed from the clubhouse, group after group on the 18th green missing one makeable putt after another. Do you also miss these makeable putts? You don't have to. Putting is too valuable a portion of the game for you to believe, as many golfers do, that great putters are born, not made. I am here to tell you that great putters are made. . . *not* born. And that you, yes you, can improve your putting dramatically.

I realized long ago that putting involves multiple talents. Reading of the greens, posture and set-up characteristics, rhythm, and stroke mechanics are all important ingredients. And there is another factor that is usually overlooked or ignored, because it involves an area about which many teachers know little. That is, how you "see" the alignment of your putter blade.

Even with what seems like abundant practice, most players never rise to their next level of performance or confidence. In July of 1992, I had the opportunity to observe the performance laboratory of Dr. Craig Farnsworth when I was giving a clinic at Cherry Hills Country Club in Denver, Colorado. Dr. Farnsworth and I have a common passion: We both yearn to make golfers score better through improved

putting. His laboratory looked like a video arcade of high tech instruments designed to improve "Visual Performance." It was truly, pun intended, an eye-opening experience.

Fortunately for you, many of Dr. Farnsworth's putting keys have been included in *See It & Sink It: Mastering Putting Through Peak Visual Performance*. I heartily suggest you read, digest, and internalize the recommendations and techniques contained in this book. I think you're in for a special treat, because you'll soon "see" ways to improve your putting.

DAVE PELZ

Prologue

Confidence is playing with your eyes.

Dr. Bob Rotella in *Golf Is a Game of Confidence*

"Mr. Farnsworth, you are on the first tee with Mr. Louis." Hearing this announcement over the public-address system, I sauntered to the tee with my low-handicapper's cockiness, eager to show another stranger how good a player I was. Within moments, my self-assured smile was replaced by a dazed look that remained on my face for hours after. It began when I shook hands and heard the words: "Hi, I'm Joe Louis."

When I look back at memorable times on the golf course, playing with the former heavyweight champion of the world in Denver, Colorado, some 25 years ago, ranks right up there.

It didn't take long for me to appreciate that, once a champion, always a champion. For the record, I don't mean he punched me out. His KOs were reserved for the greens. On the first hole he made a fifteen-foot putt. On the second hole he made an eighteen-footer. And so it went. He would scrutinize the situation, quickly approach the ball, place his putter down, and strike. I don't remember a putt he missed! Watching putt after putt go down, with a stance and stroke that would make golf teachers cringe, I became aware that Mr. Louis had transferred to the golf course that something special he once displayed in

the ring. His ability to aim to the target and sense the proper speed were special skills. Just after he sank a twenty-footer on the 9th hole, he said, "Well, I've got to catch a plane to Vegas. Thank you for letting me play with you." And Joe Louis was off to his temporary, later permanent, job as a greeter at one of Las Vegas' major casinos.

The heavyweight putting skills Joe Louis displayed that day had a profound effect on me. In time, I found myself face to face with an overlooked reason for his greatness in the ring. In effect, those nine holes with the legendary boxer laid the foundation for what would be a monumental change in my entire philosophy regarding athletic performance. They allowed me to discover that all great champions, including Joe Louis, have the *eye of a champion.*

To arrive at the Louis approach to performance in putting, I had to sift through the smoke and slogans of present-day golf's philosophers and educators. Joe Louis had learned that performance is a stimulus-response relationship. The breakthrough came with the realization that the crucial stimulus before any putt is *visual;* it's a matter of what you see, not what you feel!

Putting, like most sports performances, begins and ends with what we see and what we perceive. This statement forms the foundation for the concept of *visual dominance.* This concept becomes more basic than mechanics of the stroke, equipment, grip or stance.

The Farnsworth System is based on the fact that in order to excel on the green one must develop accurate and enduring visual performance skills such as: aiming accuracy, target localization, accuracy of visualization, space matching, visual discrimination, and visual concentration, to name a few that become the basics of perception necessary to align properly, judge distances and read the greens.

Joe Louis learned on his own that visual skills, not textbook techniques, were the keys to putting. The elite putters have these skills, and so can you. Stay tuned to acquire the *eye of a champion.*

1

Perception and the U-Factor

All knowledge has its origin in our perception.

LEONARDO DA VINCI

WHEN I FIRST tested Nick Faldo, at the Leadbetter Academy at Lake Nona Golf Club in Orlando, Florida, he was amazed that the visual perception tests he did in a hotel room could so well predict his alignment problems without there being a putter in his hands. He readily agreed with my concept of vision being *the* controlling factor in putting.

Ever wonder why you like downhill putts more than uphill putts, you miss long putts on the same side of the hole, you misalign your body and putterblade, you miss short putts?

You may be amazed, like Nick, that each of these problems is often the result of your visual perception.

The PGA Tour players I test, or interact with, are convinced a faulty stroke is the common cause of missed putts. But after going through perceptual testing, they realize the problem more often rests with the quality of their perceptions. To test your perceptions, make a dot near, but not in, opposite diagonal corners on a plain sheet of paper. Turn the paper so that the two dots appear in

After placing dots on opposite corners, make a straight line aimed toward the far dot.

While mimicking the "address" position, make a straight line pointing toward the far dot.

line as you look from behind one dot. Now, using a ruler or straight edge, draw a two-inch line, aiming it at the far dot, with one inch of the line behind the near dot and the other inch extended toward the far dot. You cannot use the ruler or paper edge beyond one inch of the dot. No fudging. Go ahead, draw it.

Before checking your results, repeat the test on another piece of paper—but this time draw the line from arm's length and to the side. In other words, mimic your perspective when aligning from over the ball.

How does it look? Are you on line? To check your accuracy in both tests, continue drawing the lines out to the far dots using a straight edge. The first test evaluates your

ability to aim at a target; the second gauges how you adjust to golf's unusual and unnatural address position beside the ball.

If either line was off even a little, imagine the error being compounded by five- to tenfold or more, as you align to a spot a few feet in front of the ball, or worse if aligning to a far target. For example, if you aimed your putter at the hole on a ten-foot putt, a one-half-inch error (at ten inches) would be compounded to a six-inch error for a ten-foot putt, when using the hole to align to. This is arrived at knowing ten feet equals 120 inches, or twelve times the test distance. Thus twelve times a one-half-inch test error equals six inches.

If you were off by more than a quarter inch when making your line from behind the dot, you can be aligning outside the hole from a distance as close as five to ten feet. If your error was worse when above the page (at address), then you compound your basic error. If not, you may have learned to compensate, in part, when over the ball. A great majority of those we tested had more of an error with the test that approximates your visual challenge in the address position. This is often because the eyes are "skewed" at the address position. In order to avoid confusion on this concept, realize that you can see something clearly but not be pointing your eyes right at it. One thing is clear—alignment is a visual challenge.

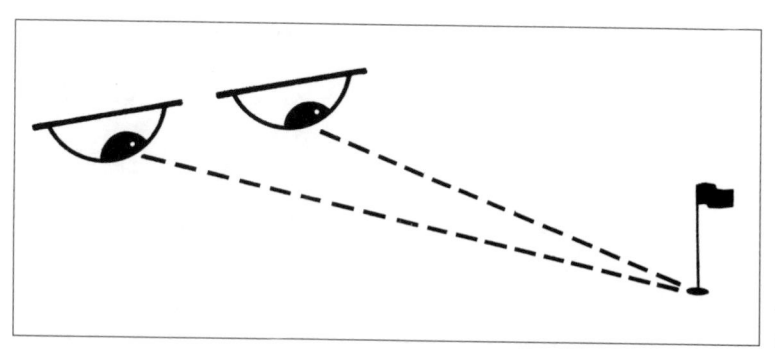

The eyes are "skewed" as they look down the line in the address position.

Another self-test that can provide information about how you perceive distance is a simple one. With a nickel or quarter in hand, place another coin that will act as a target on the floor. Pace off ten feet from the target. Face the target, close your eyes, and toss the coin in your hand at the target on the floor. Toss underhanded and attempt to land on the other coin. Before the coin lands, open your eyes to see the result. Another test is to close your eyes and walk toward a target on the floor several feet away. Once you believe you are in front of the target, drop a coin (held in your hand) on the target. Before it hits, open your eyes to see where the coin lands. It is important not to count steps as you walk. Attempt to visualize the target's location as you walk toward it with your natural step. During the "International" golf tournament, Andrew Magee reacted to the results of the dot-to-dot and walking-to-a-spot-with-eyes-closed tests by saying, "That's me, always short and left."

Scoring of these tests should be with two areas in mind. You should record what, if any, error you made to the left or right (directional) of the target and/or short or long (spatial). If you do both tests, record the highest error in each of the categories or the test that best approximates what you believe to be your typical error when putting.

There are more sophisticated tests to determine the extent

The eyes can be easily tricked. This Mueller-Lyle illusion challenges you to find which line is longer. Answer: Neither.

and the type of error, but the tests you just performed aren't bad indicators. Also realize that your perceptions can change day to day. The better putters on the PGA tour were the most accurate when undergoing an alignment test (using an infrared testing device) than the tour's statistically inferior putters. In one test of professional golfers, only eighteen percent of those who participated were accurate at aligning both behind the ball and at address.

The eyes and brain aren't as exact in their perceptual analysis as we would like to believe. Alignment and even the task of correctly judging the factors that affect the speed of the ball are two areas that are perception-based. Misperceptions can result in your eyes and brain projecting the hole to the left or right and/or short or long of its actual location. If you do not believe the above tests are a good indicator of your putts, feel free to take the "self-assessment" test in Appendix B.

Your Perceptual Challenges on the Green

It is important to determine whether any of your problems on the green are sensory—the fault of a misperception—or from a mechanical flaw, due to a poor stroke and nothing else. A majority of golfers we have tested have sensory errors at the root of their putting inconsistencies.

The perceptions we are most concerned with in putting revolve around the X-, Y- and Z-axes.

The X-axis pertains to our ability to perceive any slope or grain that can result in a putt breaking off line to the right or left. Personal X-axis misperceptions (aiming or alignment perspective) can result in faulty alignment right or left of the intended target.

Perception of the Y-axis relates to accurate estimation of the degree of elevation, or slope, of the green from the ball to the hole.

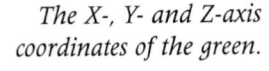

The X-, Y- and Z-axis coordinates of the green.

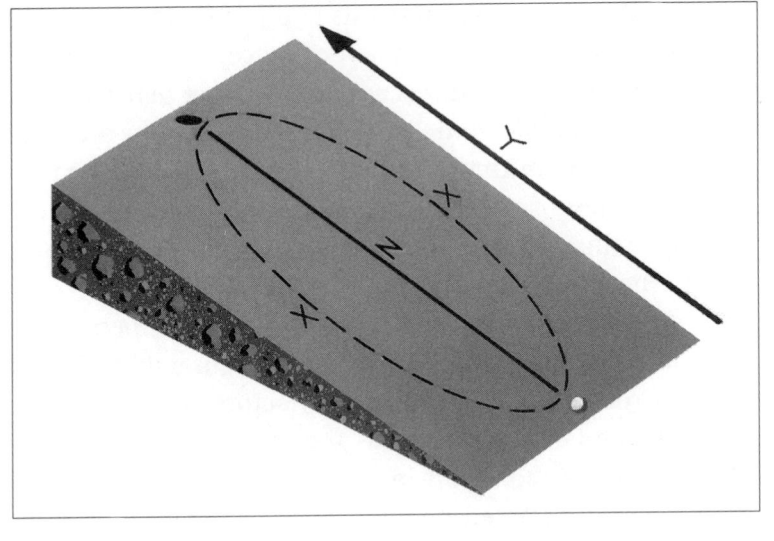

Z-axis perception is based on the ability of the two eyes to team efficiently together to perceive the true distance from the ball to the target.

For elite professionals, looking at the putt and getting a feel for it is often adequate. For them, experience is frequently a great teacher. They respond according to what they see, and the result is a made putt. They write books about how they did it, with a special technique or so. But there is one major flaw in all of this: We are assuming that our perceptions are all the same. And this can't possibly be so. No two people share the same viewpoint when interpreting the environment. Based on our own personal interactions, bias and so on, we all create our own way of interpreting the world around us.

If the eyes are not exact in what they see or perceive, no amount of emphasis on mechanics or otherwise will make up for visual inadequacies of misreading a green, or misperceiving the alignment and the speed necessary. As you will soon appreciate, the key is to know how to overcome any misperceptions.

X-axis Misperceptions

You have a *directional* misperception if your tosses or dot-to-dot drawing (or putts) were left or right of the target. This X-axis misperception error can affect your ability to aim accurately, as you are behind the ball. Quite often, this is because of the mis-teaming of the two eyes. Where the visual axes of the eyes "triangulate" (intersect) is where the target is likely to be projected by the brain. An example of aiming would be to pick an accurate spot in front of the ball and in line with the distant target as you stand behind the ball. Where you tend to aim would depend upon where your eyes perceive the target to be. Even in the address position, the accuracy of your aiming perception affects your alignment.

Those who misperceive objects left of where they actually are, tend to aim left of the target. If you were right with your tosses, you tend to aim right of the target. Most people misperceive space to the right of actual, preferring putts that break right to left rather than left-to-right breaking ones. This could well be because their alignment gives them less chance for error on right-breaking putts.

Obviously, many factors may be influencing your putting results, including experience, compensations, the ability to read greens and so forth. But the true core for your putting inconsistencies may be more basic. Your aiming tendencies may add to or negate your alignment perspective.

By far, the majority of golfers have difficulty with alignment at the address position (alignment perspective) because of the very nature of the built-in visual skew when they're at address beside the ball.

If your customary putting alignment is the opposite of your test error, it could be because a closed or open putterface looks square, or you could have learned to

compensate, for example, by closing the clubface because your putts always go right of the hole.

Z-axis Misperceptions

A *spatial* error affects your perception of distance. If you were short on your tosses or when you walked with your eyes closed, you tend toward perceiving the hole *closer* than it is in reality—a Z-axis misperception. This misperception often occurs because the eyes feed the brain with information on the target's location based on triangulation of the eye muscles. This is the way you have built your perceptual world, and this is the signal you give your motor system. To you, a distance of ten feet could be perceived as eight feet. You have created an illusion that is two feet short of reality, and the illusion becomes your real target.

If you visually constrict space, the result will be a tendency to leave your putts and chips short of the hole. This error becomes a sensory error: primarily from a faulty stimulus of your visual perception, and not from a faulty stroke. Once the stimulus is faulty, a change in your stroke or a new putter cannot alter the misperception. Without accurate perception, you'll have as much luck as a person who is trying to get a size four outfit on a size ten body. It just won't fit the circumstances.

If you are long on your tosses or the walk-the-distance test, you tend to expand space. Likewise, your putting and chipping often carries you beyond the hole, because you misperceive the hole to be beyond its actual location.

Most importantly, please realize perceptions can change. Reasons include the following:

1. Upper-back and neck problems. These areas are directly tied to your ability to accurately localize distant targets.

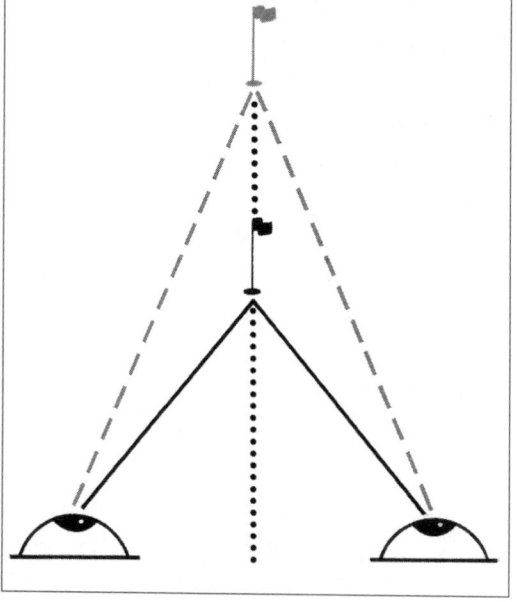

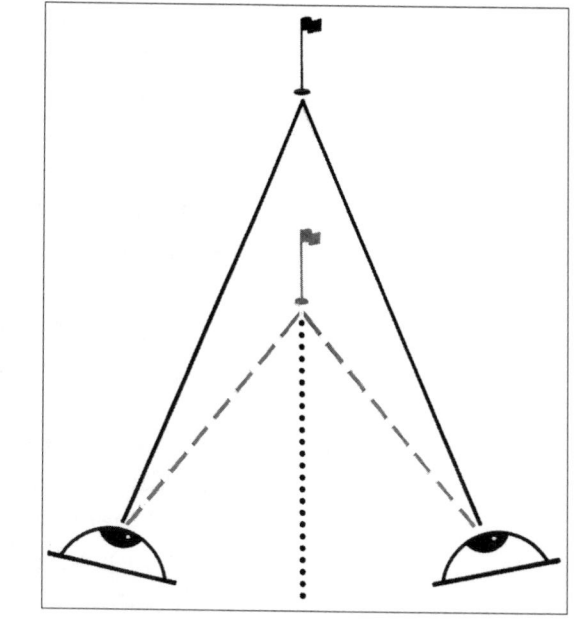

These eyes perceive the target beyond its actual location.

These eyes learned to point not at a distant target but in front of it, resulting in a misperception that is short of actual.

2. Heavy amounts of close work, including computer work, writing, or excessive reading without taking a break. This work can disrupt the usual muscle balance of the eyes, leading to eye misalignment.
3. Unstable binocularity (muscle imbalances of the two eyes).

Research has found that the elite putters have consistent eye alignment, while others have much more test-to-test variances. Even if the elite show eye imbalances, they are better able to compensate for them because they are fixed instead of constant variables. We recommend you evaluate your current perception often and keep records of your results.

Of course, our perception is infinitely more complex

than to be broken down into a few components. But perceptions are too often based on uncontrolled experiences and random or unstructured learning. If learning is not controlled, it is left to chance. The focus of this guidebook is to not leave learning to chance.

Aldous Huxley said, "Experience isn't what happens to you. It is what you do with what happens to you." I have a saying: *Those who learn to maximize their experiences get ten years' experience ten times. Those who let it be just another event of life without extracting meaning from it—without the awareness necessary—will tend to get one year's experience ten times.* In other words, they will tend to repeat the same old pattern and the same old mistakes.

The brain must be given as much information as possible that is relevant to the putt. For nearly a century, since Ivan Pavlov's discovery, scientists have known the brain can recircuit itself when presented with consistent changes in stimuli.

The sensory challenge of putting requires the brain to receive accurate visual stimuli. When the stimulus is picked up by the eyes, it is transferred to the brain for interpretation, and the motor (muscle) system is programmed to respond appropriately. For some, this connection needs only a little tuning for them to excel. For the majority, it will take time and repetition to establish an accurate "eye-mind-body loop."

Misperceptions can also be the causal factor for a poor stroke. Those who perceive the target as right of actual, learn to get the ball near the hole by using a compensating out-to-in stroke. This subconscious attempt to correct for the misperception creates a lateral spin on the ball. This isn't how the stroke was taught, but how powerful misperceptions can be.

The better putters impart a minimum degree of sidespin on the ball because their stroke path is more straight back and through and their blade more square at impact than

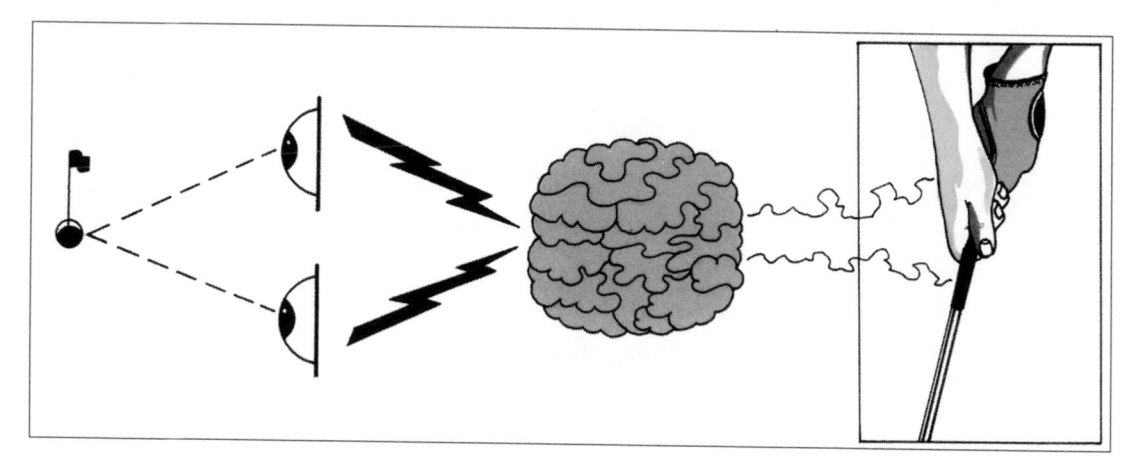

The eyes-to-mind-to-body "loop" in putting.

those who need to change their swing path to compensate for visual misperceptions.

Joe Louis had the eye of a champion. And you can, too. Once we learn how to see and perceive accurately, all that follows will take on an orderly sequence resulting in positive action. The major point: Perceptions can be altered. The first step to this change deals with awareness. Awareness of what the elite of all sports have in common—*visual dominance*.

2

Mastering Green Reading

When you can't center your eyes, you can't quiet your mind, and you need that quiet for your concentration.

LPGA'S VAL SKINNER

READING THE CHARACTERISTICS of the green before you putt can be the origination of a great finish or the beginning of a disaster. To be a better green-reader, one should start with an understanding of the concept of *visual dominance*.

Visual dominance is based on the belief that almost everything we do begins with what we see or what we perceive. This concept promotes the belief that the visual sensory system should be the lead system, the controlling system, for most performance—especially in sports. In other words, the brain needs to focus primarily on visual stimuli and relegate other sensory information. This includes moving the mechanics so highly promoted by the game of golf, primarily to the background when on the course and especially when on the greens. Green reading is primarily a visual challenge.

The specialty of optometry has emphasized for some time the importance of the anatomical and physiological connection of the eyes and the brain. A sports scientist at

the U.S. Olympic Training Center in Colorado Springs called visual dominance "possibly the last frontier of performance enhancement."

When the ski instructor says to "look down the slope" or the Bondurant Racing School instructs its drivers to get their eyes to the next turn while they are still in a preceding turn, they are stressing to *let the eyes lead the body.*

The determinant to ultimately trusting the eyes to lead the action lies with the accuracy of the visual performance skills that are primary to the sport. The superstars of putting have honed the accuracy of such visual skills as *depth perception, target localization, visualization accuracy, peripheral awareness, visual discrimination, vision-balance integration, eye-hand coordination* and other similar skills paramount to performance. Thus the label, visual performance skills.

These performance skills separate golf's acknowledged great putters—Ben Crenshaw, Brad Faxon, Paul Runyan, Jack Nicklaus, Bobby Locke, Isao Aoki and Dave Stockton—from the rest. Does this statement mean that mechanics takes a backseat in putting? Yes, it does.

The great putter's stroke and blade are like vehicles that power the ball toward a certain point or target. But the vehicle can't find its way without the visual performance skills responsible for reading the greens, aligning one's body to the target and powering the ball the correct distance to the hole along a given path.

This book focuses on developing visual guidance tools to achieve at the next level. Realize, just playing the game will not allow you to develop all the basic visual skills of performance. As will be seen, visual dominance is the most complete physiologically efficient pattern of functioning to meet the demands of putting, including even the stroke itself.

Visual dominance includes the *outer* and the *inner* eye. (The inner eye's role in mastering the challenge of dis-

tance is discussed in Chapter Eight.) In golf the outer eye serves three main purposes. First, it is your chief ally to read the green. Second, it is your range finder. It gives the brain accurate or inaccurate information as to the location of the target for alignment. Third, it is your greatest link to your environment by serving as your best ambassador to the present. You must recognize and coordinate these three aspects in order to consistently enjoy success.

This chapter focuses on ways to develop a better outer eye for green-reading skills. One of my favorite sayings— *You must know what to look for or you won't see it, even when you look right at it*—is quite applicable when it comes to green reading. No matter how good your stroke or on target your alignment, if you don't *see* the green's read, the putt is a lost cause.

The Farnsworth System Analysis

The nine key steps to becoming a better green reader are:

1. Obtain information from knowledgeable locals.
2. Putt from every possible place on the practice green using the information you have heard, combined with what you see.
3. Observe the terrain as you approach the greens on the course.
4. Note the slope and drainage surrounding the green.
5. Divide the green into fourths.
6. Observe the green from the best perspective to assess the degree of slope.
7. Observe any nuances in your immediate section.
8. Pay particular attention to the last few feet of the ball's intended path and the slope behind the hole.
9. Make green reading an art by studying all the factors that can affect the ball's roll, such as grain and slope. This includes a special lesson from your golf professional.

The following is a step-by-step procedure to arrive at a decision before attempting to putt.

1. Tour players have a keen eye when it comes to assessing slope and grain, but even they can gain more knowledge by asking questions from knowledgeable people that can save them time (and strokes). You can gain the same "instant" knowledge if you ask the right questions.

I encourage my players to write to or interview the home golf pro in advance for a green-by-green synopsis, such as what lakes, terrain or other factors can affect the ball's roll. For the amateur, it isn't a crime to inquire of the pro shop personnel and those you encounter on the putting green. Ask questions such as, "Are there greens where I must avoid attacking the pin or keep the ball away from a severe downslope?"

2. Spend quality time on the practice green. Find how much the grain affects the ball's roll. Find out, too, if the slope makes uphill putts really slow down as they approach the hole and really run with downhillers. Determine if adjustments are needed for the uphill or downhill putts compared with your home course. Spend time with moderate to long practice putts (fifteen to twenty of them).

3. You are playing your first round at Arrowhead Golf Course, outside of Denver. Your inquiry uncovered that the course is short and tight. Firsthand knowledge of the greens is paramount. "Everything breaks away from the foothills," you hear from the locals.

The proper visual perspective for green reading can be gained by knowing where and what to look for as well as how to look. You notice as you approach the second green that there is quite a drop off from the left side of the green to the right. You are also aware of the green's proximity to the foothills, and you surmise (correctly) that the grain and slope may be prominent. Your fairway

The second green at Arrowhead, in the foothills outside Denver, Colorado.

shot is directed by the obvious: The foothills are left of the green. So you aim your shot right of the pin to give yourself an uphill putt instead of a potential slick downhiller.

The question of where to look arises as you approach the green. For most layouts, I recommend obtaining a perspective from approximately forty to fifty yards away from the green. Other times it can be helpful to start your observation much sooner. Another good rule of thumb is that 90 percent of the greens slope from back to front.

4. Knowing how to "look" involves what I call taking a *wide perspective*. For this the eyes must learn to look "easy."

An expanded view near the green can yield clues not readily appreciated when on the green.

By taking in a wider field of view, instead of a hard or intense look, the eyes have a better chance of seeing the proper perspective of the degree of slope that may affect the ball's roll on the green.

On the green, the player has a reduced perspective of the surrounding terrain that can affect the ball's roll. Another good rule is to stand far enough off the green so as to see the entire green without any eye movement.

A green such as the second at Arrowhead has a distinctive drainage area that causes the grain to flow with the slope. A subtle slope may possibly be countered by a lake or pond that draws the grain's growth the opposite way of the slope. But a moderate and a severe slope will always have the grain growing with the slope because of the drainage. This creates a situation that should alert the golfer to play even more break than is seen.

5. Pay attention to the sections of the green:

- Divide the green into fourths.
- Determine if the surrounding terrain influences the ball's roll.
- Determine what section affects the ball's roll the most.
- Determine what section affects the ball's roll the next most.

Typically, if the greens are familiar and the pin placements are known, I prefer my students to divide the green into fourths. First, it helps them plan their club selection and direction of aim for their approach shot. This is important because some pin positions invite disaster if the player is not aware. For instance, a certain green may be so severely sloped that from anywhere above the hole the player is going to be fortunate to two-putt. He or she would be more fortunate to just be on the fringe short of the hole than on the green above the hole. The same applies if, for example, the pin is on the right side, near a left-to-right slope in the middle of the green. The player does not want the ball to land left of the hole. Secondly, sectioning the green can yield a better assessment of the characteristics of the green.

If the terrain surrounding the green is fairly steep, an optical illusion can make a mildly sloped green look level, especially as the player gets close to the green. Be aware of this potential situation. Also, the more the surrounding terrain slopes, the more the grain will tend to go toward the low area of the terrain.

The greenside perspective does not mean that the situation will be entirely the same once on the green, as there can be depressions in sections of the green that do not relate to the surrounding terrain or the overall slope. The overall perspective must include visual clues of slope and grain made when on the green. For instance, you hit your fairway shot from 165 yards out to a green that appears to slope towards the fairway. You notice there is a moderate slope descending from your position to the green. As you get within twenty yards of the green, the terrain from the sides and the back of the green do not change your mind about the slope being a gentle one going from back to front. You surmise the grain will go the same, back to front. Your ball landed behind the pin by twenty-five feet.

You allow for the grain and slope going with you. You stroke the ball and come up six feet short. What happened? Unfortunately, you forgot to factor in greenside observation with what you had observed when you were 165 yards out. The overall perspective of the slope being back to front was negligible. The putt became more level than downhill. The lesson is, take in all the information as well as realize that the designers of the course use such subtleties to visually trick you. Make sure you don't reach a final decision before you get a reading on the green.

When you use the wide view as you approach the green, you have a better chance of factoring in this next point. If the green has a subtle to mild slope, and the slope matches the direction of the slope of the surrounding terrain, the break will usually be more than is seen on the green. If the slope is opposite of the surrounding terrain, play less break than is seen. If the slope is moderate to severe, no matter the surrounding terrain, the general rule of thumb is to play it for more break than you see.

6. Standing near greenside, you should assess the green's degree of slope off to the side and halfway from its front to back for a green that slopes front to back or vice versa. If the green slopes left to right, or vice versa, then

Visual perspectives near the green afford a better view of the slope.

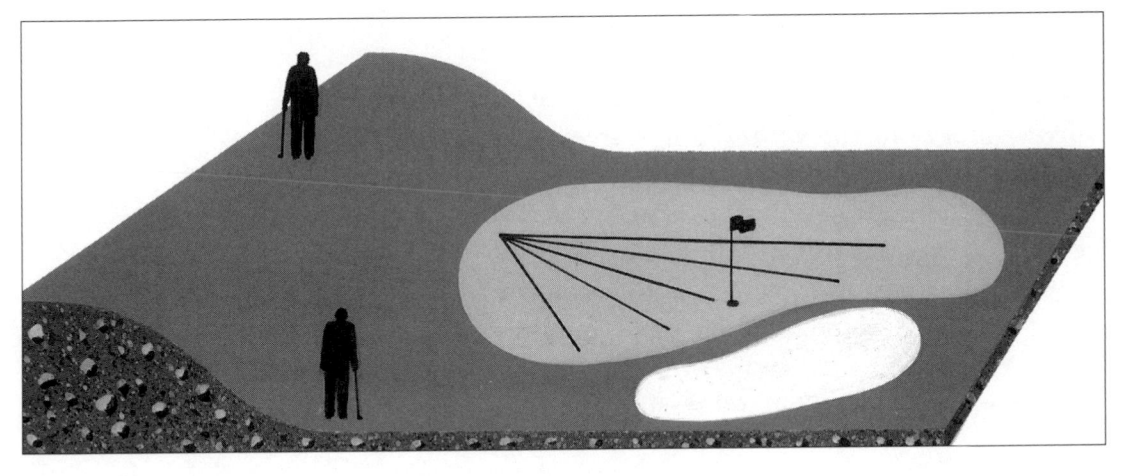

standing in front of or behind the green can give you a better visual assessment of the degree of slope. Possibly, you may need to do both.

7. The next step is to analyze the sections of the green your ball will travel in. We label this your immediate section. In this case, your ball will travel in the right two sections (the back right to the front right). As you walk near the path the ball will need to travel, you assess the slope and compare it section to section.

Determine whether the section your ball is in is more sloped than the section the hole is in, or vice versa. The reason for this assessment: The ball's roll is less affected when it is moving fast off the putter. When the ball starts to slow down, the green's characteristics of grain and slope have more effect.

A good visual aid as you stand at the highest point on the green is to imagine slowly pouring a bucket of water

The immediate section encompasses all of the ball's path to the hole.

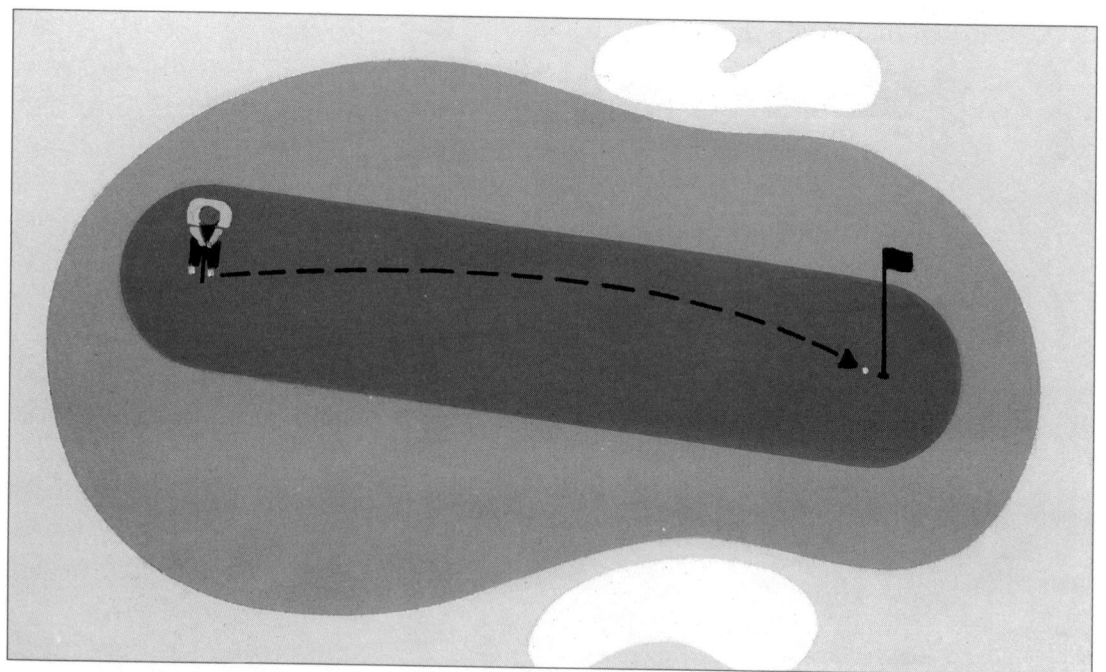

onto the green. Picture where the water would flow. Note how this would affect the ball's roll.

In Chapter Eight, you will better appreciate the degrees of slope and what affect will be seen depending on where the slope lies in different sections of the ball's roll.

8. You now fine-tune sectioning even more by observing the last three or four feet the ball will roll in front of the hole and the area immediately behind the hole. I cannot emphasize enough the necessity to take a look from behind the hole, especially on downhill putts. This is often a much better perspective than from behind the ball. For your putt, the slope is moderate and the grain is moderate, including the area behind the hole. You see that you cannot charge the putt because of the slope and grain going with the (eventual) path of the ball. You see the hole has a worn area on its downside, telling you that previous putts are hitting that area repeatedly.

The last few feet are where the ball's roll may be influenced the most.

9. Before you pull the trigger, the brain must make a decision or the motor system will not render a confident stroke. It is time to put all of your information together. By taking in as much relevant information as possible, the decision of any break, and how much,

can be made easier. By continuing to train the outer eye, it will eventually see even the subtlest of slopes.

In summary, the most important section to read is often where the hole resides, because it has the most influence on the ball's roll. The next most influential section is where the green's slope and grain will affect the ball when it starts to slow down, most often near the midway point of the entire roll.

Now we must concern ourselves with training the eyes to look for the clues on the green. Here comes a great start.

The Basics

Becoming a good-to-great putter starts with your ability to read the green's characteristics. The green characteristics that can influence the ball's roll are:

Slope

The slope can have the most profound effect of all on the ball's speed and direction. The slope can sling the ball right or left of the hole (X-axis factor) or cause the ball to slow quite quickly when going uphill or speed downhill as if it were never going to stop (Y-axis factor). Slopes can have different effects on the ball depending on the speed of the ball when it encounters the undulation (Z-axis factor). The rules of the slope are:

1. Uphill putts add to the effective distance of the putt compared with a level putt because of gravity pushing against the ball.
2. Downhill putts reduce the effective distance because gravity slings it farther than if it were a level surface.
3. The more the slope, the more the ball's roll will be affected.

4. The faster the ball speed (slow greens), the less effect of the slope.

5. A slope near the origination of the putt will have less effect than when the slope is near the hole.

6. The shorter the cut of grass (a fast green), the more the slope will affect the break, because the ball's speed is slower.

7. Sidehill putts tend to sling the ball farther left or right than most expect, often because the ball speed is less. Think of the slope as a vector that points the ball in the downhill direction of the slope.

Chapter Eight will cover ways and means to handle the challenges of the slope, especially the first two points above. For now, it is important to develop the outer eye to recognize the degrees of slopes and other keys to help you be more aware on the greens.

The more the slope, the greater the effect on the ball's roll. The degrees of slope are categorized as mild, moderate and severe.

A *mild* slope is a slope that shows very little drop from its highest to its lowest point. It is, at the most, a subtle drop of a foot or less. The effect of the mild slope is minimal compared with the other degrees, but a fast green can turn

Mild, moderate and severe slopes.

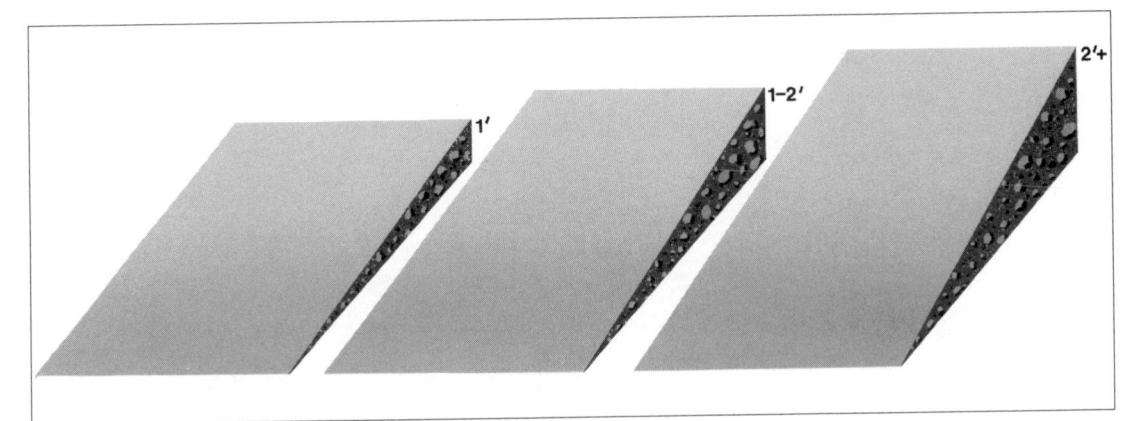

a mild slope into a moderate slope, resulting in the necessity to play more break.

A *moderate* slope shows a difference of one to two feet from its highest to lowest point. It can moderately affect the ball's roll whether it be a right-to-left (X-axis) break or vice versa or an uphill or downhill (Y-axis) slope. This means the ball will break more than a mild slope if putting across the slope, possibly up to three or four feet.

A *severe* slope must be recognized, for it can harshly affect how the X- and Y- axes read. A severe slope shows an elevation difference of more than two feet from the highest to the lowest point. The more severe the slope the more important it is to position your approach shot to avoid facing a slick downhiller with no chance to stop it within two or three feet of the hole if you miss. On a severe slope, when putting sidehill, a good rule is to always play for more break than is seen. The reason: Because of the green's speed, the ball will travel slower over the surface, allowing for more "grab" by the slope and grain on the ball. A severe slope can mean a break of five, ten or more feet.

One of the little used techniques to detect green subtleties is observing a green during dusk, where the hidden contours are often highlighted when the light is filtered. The green now reveals subtle areas that aren't so recognizable by the human eye during a bright day.

GRAIN

Grain is the direction the grass grows. This can cause friction against the ball when putting *into* the grain. The ball sort of floats over the grain when putting *with* the grain's flow. The green's grain can affect the roll of the ball almost as much as a mild slope, and it can turn a mild slope into a severe slope if the grain grows in the direction of the slope. Conversely, the grain can diminish the effects of the slope if it runs counter to the slope (possible with mild slopes).

Looking at the cup's edge may give you a clue as to where the balls are hitting the edge. A worn edge means the balls are breaking toward the mark (from the cup's center).

To determine the grain's direction:

1. Look to see whether the green or surrounding terrain has a clear direction to it—grain will grow toward low areas.
2. Look to see whether the green has a shiny appearance (down grain) or a dull appearance (against the grain).
3. Look around the hole or the edge of the green.
4. Look for nearby water that the grain will grow toward.

If not recognized, the grain's effect can leave a long comeback putt. What looked like a flat twenty-five footer, if against the grain, may leave a second putt that is five or six feet short of the hole (because of the slowing effect of the grain). A downhill slope with the grain may leave you well past the hole. With the same putt, if the grain grew against you and the grain wasn't factored, you could face a testy downhiller for your second putt.

The grain's direction can be influenced by the shade of a tree, the mower pushing the grass down or a nearby lake. Grain tends to grow in the direction of the water runoff, toward the lowest point on the green, the surrounding terrain or a nearby pond or lake.

Water could be a few miles to many miles away and still have an influence on the putt. Bermuda greens, often found in the South or in warmer climates, feature thicker grain and can be more of a factor than Bent grass, often found in the Northern states. Bermuda grass also tends to grow from east to west, following the sun's daily path. Local prevailing winds can push grain down in the direction it typically blows toward. Bent grass is often cut so low, to avoid damage to the roots, that it is of little factor in putting.

Look for clues as you approach the green. As you fine-tune your outer eye to observe the grain along the path of your putt, realize that grain may not always grow the same way over the entire green. Also, it's helpful to observe the second cut of the green's collar where the length of the grass may better show the direction of the grain in a particular area. The rules of the grain are:

1. The longer the cut of grass, the less the affect the break (X-axis factor). Play less break when putting across a slope.
2. The shorter the cut, the more the slope can affect the break.
3. Putting into the grain can add to the overall distance effect (Y-axis). A fifteen-foot putt may play like an eighteen footer.
4. Putting with the grain can decrease the overall distance effect of the putt. A twenty-footer may play like a twelve-footer.

A slope can be countered by the grain's path.

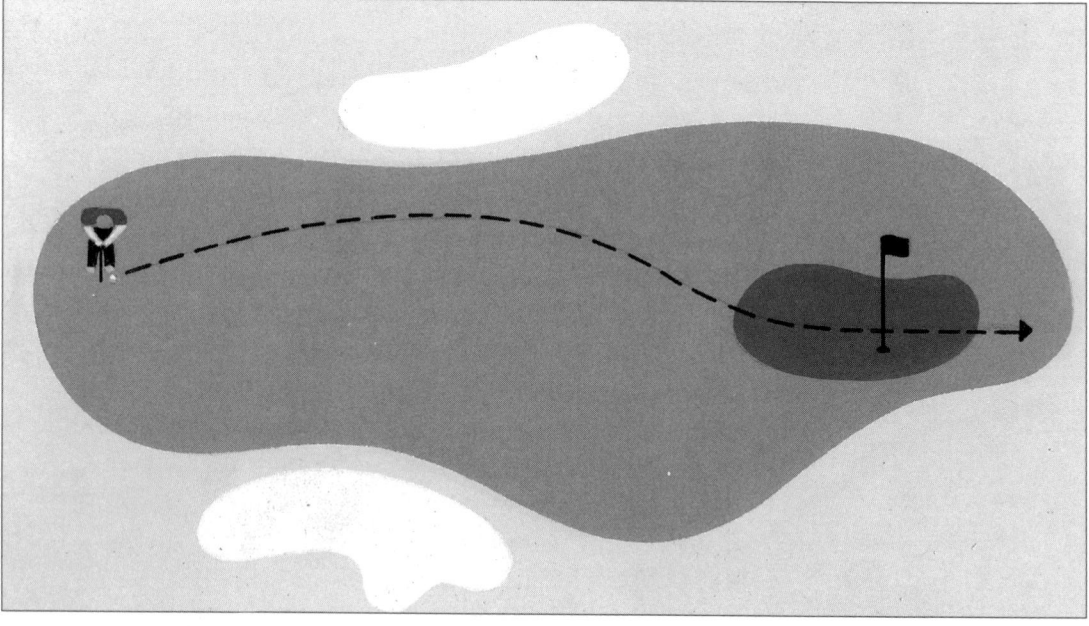

The green's grain tends to grow toward a nearby lake or pond.

5. Putting across the grain will add to the break.

A factor your outer eye must compute is the green's condition. Green speed will affect your aim. The slower the green, the faster the ball will need to be propelled and the less the grain will affect the break. A fast green means the ball will not be traveling as fast off the putterface, so the slope has more influence, forcing you to play for more break. A slow green may make a twenty-foot putt play as if it were a twenty-five foot or more putt under ideal playing conditions. On the contrary, a faster green than you are used to must also change your putting strategy. A twenty-foot putt may need to be played as if were a seven- or eight-footer.

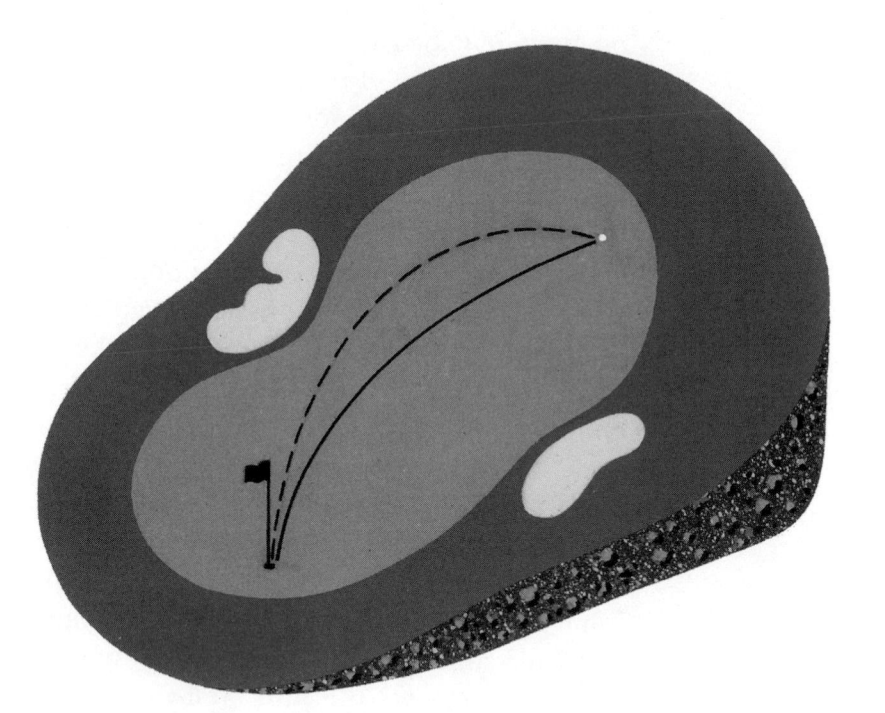

WIND

Recalling the gale force wind during the 1995 British Open at St. Andrews reminds us that strong winds can affect the ball's roll.

A fast green, with the grain cut quite short, leads to the necessity to borrow more break than if the grain were longer and the speed slower.

Seeing Through the Eyes of a Champion

During our putting clinics, one of the most helpful ways to gain a discriminating eye was when the students went out on several greens with their golf professional. They were shown subtle to severe slopes and asked to evaluate the amount of break they saw. They were allowed to "see through a champion's eyes" when the pro told them and showed them what he saw. Importantly, all our students,

on putts that had more than a subtle break, underestimated the amount of the break.

After reading and absorbing this chapter, arrange a playing lesson with your pro for the specifics of reading greens. When you take the lesson, record his comments for future reference.

Listen to the pro's explanation of the effects of drainage, slope, wind or possibly even the setting sun's influence on the grain's direction. Take notes on his entire explanation of why the ball will roll a certain way on different parts of the green. Pay attention to how the slope and grain may enhance or counter each other's effect. Look for grain that goes across your intended path and how a seemingly straight putt demands you aim outside the hole. Discuss why grain that goes away from your position looks shiny, while grain growing at you looks dull and darker. Know that grain against your putting path slows the putt, and the opposite situation makes the ball roll farther, as if it were a downhiller. Most important, start to look for information and work to see it. Note the length, texture and thickness of the grass. Pay attention to such items as the hole's position, in front of or behind a slope, that will influence the ball's roll. Start to look for the best perspective to evaluate certain putts—above, below the hole or from the side. After you or the pro putt, closely examine the ball's roll as it travels over the green's slope and grain. It may help to imagine you are in the ball as it rolls. Appreciate the ball's speed as dependent on the green's condition.

For a particular course (other than your home course) whose greens give you fits, set up a green-reading lesson with the home pro or have your pro make arrangements if he is going to be instructing. Just knowing what the pro sees may not allow you to immediately transfer this to green after green, course after course and putt after

putt. Be patient. Don't get discouraged if you can't see everything immediately. Keep looking to *see* it. It will come. Remember, the subtleties of some greens aren't always seen, even by the elite. But in time, you should master most of the factors. You will eventually look with the champion's eye.

The inability to interpret the green's characteristics has put many a fine player off the pro tours. Yet, green reading is an acquired skill. You aren't just born with this ability. What is it that some have that others have not? The vast majority of players suffer from a lack of "visual discrimination." Either they do not know what to look for or they don't recognize the information that the green presents. In my lab, I have numerous drills to enhance this valuable performance skill.

LITTLE IDEAS OF NOTE

My father, "Dode," was a very strong man with a great putting "eye." He once discussed a point concerning reading breaks that I never forgot. I am not sure where he got the idea other than from his own experience, or why this effect takes place. His comment centered around uphill and downhill putts that appeared to have no right or left influence from the slopes. It came after I had misread an uphill putt, verbally wondering why it broke away from the hole at the last moment without any visible reason. My father's rule of thumb went as follows:

1. Uphill putts tend to break slightly to the right.
2. Downhill putts tend to break slightly to the left.

When there appear to be negligible grain or slope factors to spin it right or left of the hole, favor aiming toward

continued

the hole's left-of-center edge for an uphill putt and right-of-center edge for a downhill putt. This aiming rule may need to be altered based on your alignment tendencies, but with everything equal, use "Dode's Rule" for those uphill and downhillers.

On shorter putts, I love Corey Pavin's routine of getting down to the ground a few feet behind the ball to assess any undulations from the ball to the hole just before he addresses the ball. This is a great visual perspective.

The Dominant Eye for Aiming

It is important to know which eye is dominant—which eye is your aiming eye. As you will soon discover, this will come in handy later for certain techniques and may affect your head positioning in the address position.

Hold your hands together, forming a hole approximately the size of a quarter. Find a target several feet away from you. While looking at the target with both eyes open, quickly bring your hands up to eye level, looking through the hole you made.

A dominant eye test.

Close one eye, then the other. Whichever eye sees the target through the hole (without moving your hand or head) is your dominant eye. You will notice how much the target appears to shift as you switch from eye to eye. This disparity is important to note, because it shows you how much off line you can be if you use the wrong eye when doing certain techniques in this book.

THE PLUMB

Plumbing or plumb-bobbing is appropriately named for the plumb or chalk-line used by carpenters and plumbers to make a straight line for reference. Many golfer's utilize the putter's shaft as a "plumb" to create a straight line to help interpret deviations of elevations of the green that can affect the roll of the ball. They stand behind and in line with the ball and the hole and hold the putter so the lower shaft bisects the ball and they see if the hole, seen near the top of the shaft is right or left of the shaft. If the hole appears left of the shaft, they believe this connotes a contour of the green that will cause the ball to break from right to left.

I am going to stick my neck out here and, no doubt, cause a great deal of anxiety for the countless numbers who use the plumb for a "read" of the green's break when I state that the real reason most see any deviation of the hole to the side of the shaft is due to their subconscious, and nothing else.

In actuality, if everything was perfectly in line, the ball and hole would always be aligned on the shaft. What

really creates a situation of the hole being off the shaft starts with what golfers see. Their eyes tell them that there is a break, often based on previous knowledge or an obvious break. The players' subconscious positions them a little off line, or they tilt their heads to create an illusion of reality.

Optically, you can create this perspective by placing two golf balls eight or so feet apart on the floor at home.

continued

This putt will break right-to-left (from the shaft to the hole).

Hold your shaft up at arm's length away and in front of your dominant eye. Close the other eye. Position yourself behind and directly in line with the two balls so that you see the closer ball near the bottom of the putter shaft and the farther ball is near the top of the shaft. If you take a step to the left, then turn slightly to the right in order to place the lower ball on the bottom of the shaft, you will notice the upper ball is now to the left of the shaft. I believe this is the same perspective that the players perceive when their subconscious shifts them to the side, or they lean down the slope or even tilt their head (to create this disparity).

To all of you that use the plumb, you no doubt want to continue to incorporate this into your routine so you are comfortable. But there is no substitute for good visual awareness.

The Challenge

If more players would get away from the power myth and start making putting an art form, the average score would, for the first time in decades, take a significant dip. Get smart and spend time mastering the visual challenge of green reading by becoming a student of the greens.

1. Program the brain to accept the importance of green reading.
2. Know what to look for and ask questions about the green's conditions.
3. When approaching the green, observe the surrounding terrain.
4. Section the green.
5. Observe the green from the best position to judge the slope while off the green.
6. Look for slope and grain factors in your "immediate" section.
7. Pay particular attention to the last four feet of the ball's roll for green and slope factors.

8. Always be sure to look at the putt from below the hole.
9. From behind the ball, put together all you have observed and, if applicable, use "Dode's Rule" if all else is negligible.
10. Make a decision.
11. Schedule a green-reading lesson from your golf professional.

3

Are You a Victim of the "50 Percent Rule"?

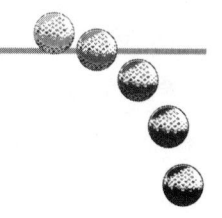

In no other game is the ratio of playing field to goal so large. We are spread so wide as we play, yet brought to a tiny place.

FROM *GOLF IN THE KINGDOM*

VISION HAS A natural reflex to overcome. The eyes naturally take in a visual field that's at least 50 percent greater than the actual size of the object of focus. The eyes expand the field, using peripheral vision, to locate where the object is in relation to other objects. This sounds like a good thing, but this natural perspective can result in an increased chance for error—what I call the 50 Percent Rule. What the eyes take in becomes the area one can hit to or aim at.

In putting, the 50 Percent Rule can increase the hole's size, from 4.25 inches to over 6 inches. So, if you aim to one side of the "expanded" hole to compensate for a break in the green, you will probably miss the putt.

The golf ball is 1.68 inches in diameter. With the 50 Percent Rule, its size increases by over half an inch (.50 X

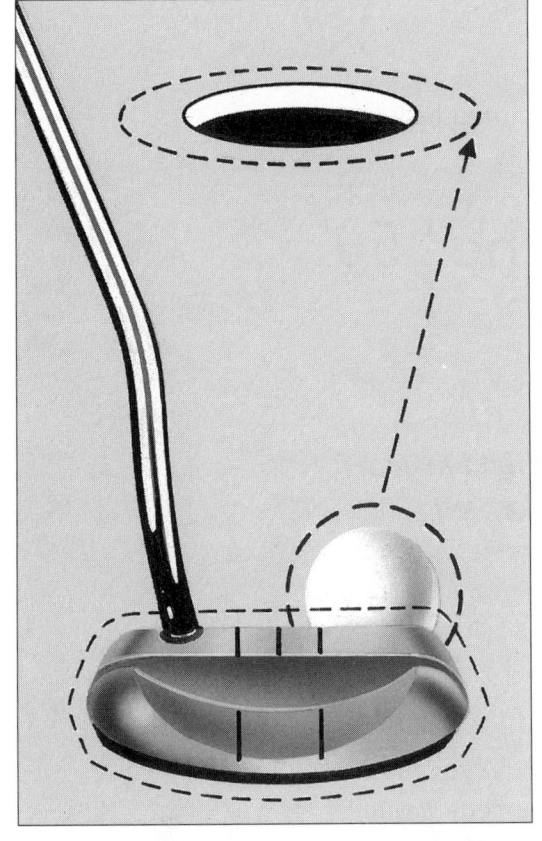

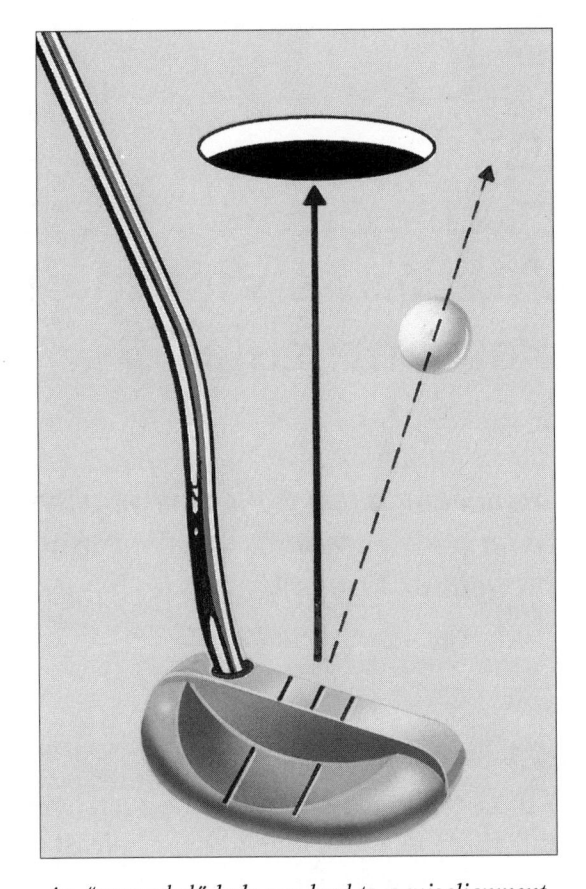

The 50 Percent Rule increases the chance for error.   *An "expanded" hole can lead to a misalignment.*

1.68 = .84). If you were inadvertently fixating on the top of the ball, adding .84 of an inch to it, you would probably top the putt. In fact, if it weren't for the depth of the putterblade, you might miss the ball completely.

If you add 50 percent to the size of the putterhead, it's possible to hit the ball with only a fraction of the face. Could the 50 Percent Rule contribute to Dave Pelz's observation that a mis-hit is a key reason why the ball does not reach its destination on long putts? You bet!

Mis-hits Can Be a Significant Cause of Error

Pelz says that a mis-hit can result in a loss of at least 20 percent of impact potential. This means the putted ball can finish several feet short of your intended target. Therefore, when you hit a putt short of the hole, ask yourself whether you are a victim of the 50 Percent Rule. In other words, did you hit the ball off-center with the toe or the heel of the club?

Obviously, the golfer can reduce his scoring average just by reducing or eliminating his mis-hits. This requires the eyes to ditch this natural way of seeing the world. In other words, one must be more visually specific.

The built-in generalities of the 50 Percent Rule leave you with too much room for error. Furthermore, the body's muscles aren't given the *fine-tuning* to respond appropriately.

A "toed" or "heeled" hit can result in a putt that does not reach the intended target.

Placing a dot on the back of the ball helps the eyes fine-tune.

To avoid the consequences of natural, untrained vision, we recommend you aim only at specific targets. For some, this emphasis on specifics may be all that is necessary to sink those putts that lip out.

To impact your ability to hit the putt squarely, aim at a specific area of dimples on the back of the ball or its back apex.

In a 1985 article in *GOLF Magazine,* Raymond Floyd said he imagines a tack on the back of the ball where he is to direct his putter. For reducing your chances of mis-hits on long putts, the "tack" is a great visual aid well worth emulating.

Fine-tuning also includes choosing an appropriate target to aim at. In order to minimize your chances for error, your distance target should be a piece of grass or a small spot.

Note:

To help you fine-tune your aim in practice, putt to a dime or tee. That way, when you set out on the course, the hole will look like a well.

Turn Your Eyes on Easy

Some players freeze over the ball when attempting to fine-tune. They focus too intently on the ball. To understand this problem, look at a letter on this page or an eyelet on one of your shoes. Look real hard for about ten seconds. You will notice that the longer you look, the more the muscles of your eyes, those in your face and those in your arms and hands tighten.

To counter this problem, and promote relaxation, "turn the eyes on easy." For best results, look at the ball in a

relaxed way until the putter starts approaching impact. At that point, fine-tune on a dimple or the back apex of the ball.

Before the stroke, make sure fine-tuning is a part of your pre-stroke routine. Practice focusing your eyes "easy" away from the course. Look with reduced effort whenever you can.

In order to avoid generalities, always choose as small a spot as possible for your target. By being specific in where you align and direct your aim, you will reduce any tendencies for the 50 Percent Rule to rear its ugly head. Being specific by looking at the grain and slope will also help you master the specific demands of the putting game.

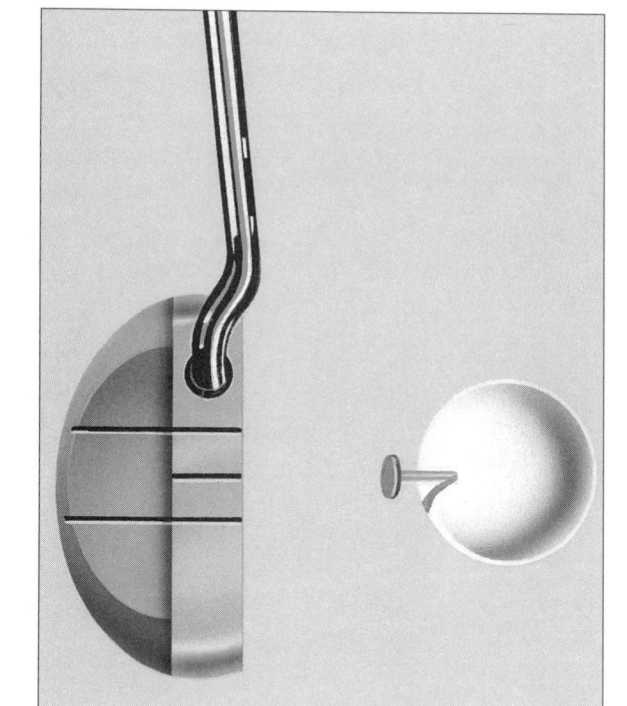

Fine-tune and nail your putts.

THE MYTH OF THE "THREE-FOOT CIRCLE"

An axiom of golf instruction claims that putting to a three-foot circle helps the player relax and make a better putt. The idea is that the enlarged target reduces the demand of the task, thus reducing the self-enforced pressure. Unfortunately, this bit of advice contains a built-in conflict with our conceptual skills. Ironically, your expectations are reduced, yet your three-putts increase. The three-foot-circle tip decreases the specifics of both direction and the spatial challenges that good putting must meet. If we use this concept, our eyes may direct the ball to go at least three feet beyond the hole.

continued

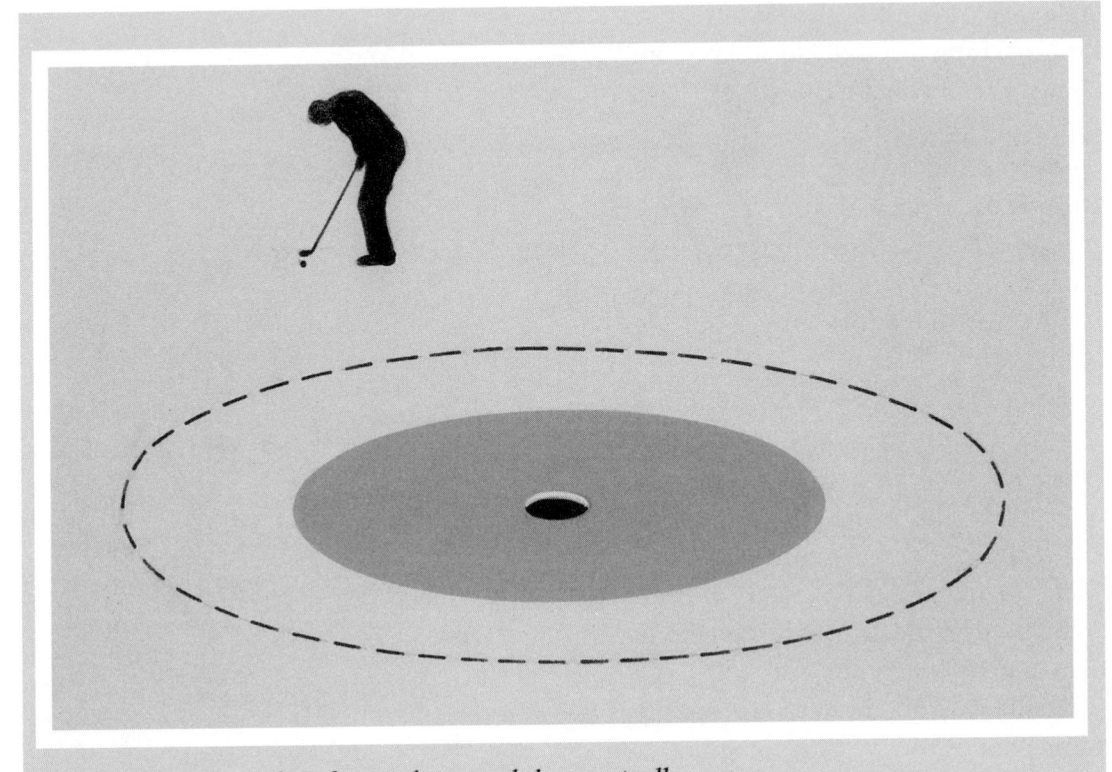

From a long distance, three feet can be expanded, perceptually.

Obviously, this problem is more severe on downhill putts.

Jesper Parnevik tested out exceptionally. But his chief complaint was an inability to handle the straight putt. Surprisingly, he had no trouble on breaking putts. We surmised that this was because, on sloping greens, he used his imagination. Furthermore, on straight putts his eyes were not fine-tuned, so he used the *whole* cup. Moral: Always pick as small a target as possible.

It doesn't take any more effort to be specific. Being specific does not require any disruption of concentration. On the contrary, it enhances it. When possible, especially on shorter putts, always pick a target as small as possible, such as a blade of grass instead of the hole.

Visual Adjustment

Henry David Thoreau once said, "The true measure of your intelligence is the flexibility of your adaptability." It pains me to hear a player say, "Those greens killed me today." The greens are not at fault. Rather the player remained ingrained with habits that did not fit the challenge. In short, he did not exercise "visual flexibility."

Day in and day out, our eyes do not give us an unchanging reference to the positions of our targets. In golf, warm-up time allows us to find out what is happening with our perception before we step to the first tee. The Farnsworth System has a rule of thumb when a player is finding it difficult to get the ball near the hole: Adopt a different target. If your putts are coming up short, pick a target farther past the hole. (Hitting it "harder" becomes too general and isn't visually directed.) If your putts finish past the hole, choose a target closer than the one you were using. These visual adjustments are the easiest (and least disruptive) to implement during play.

If you are overestimating the breaks, reduce your "read" accordingly. If you are underestimating the break, add one, two or three inches to what you see—whatever fits the circumstance. From now on, don't let visual and mental rigidity spoil an entire round. Play smart. Be *flexible*.

CLEARING THE MIND—THE PRESENT TIME TECHNIQUE

Everybody has times when they need to clear their mind. Some athletes use hypnosis. Others may incorporate breathing techniques Once again, visual dominance can come to the rescue.

A well-respected local golfer, Bob Russo, recently came from several shots back on the final day of competition to challenge for the lead in the Vail Fall Invitational. A friend of his, who

continued

was scouting the other groups, provided a constant update on how the field stood.

Bob would hear, "Smith just bogeyed; you are two in back of him. . . . Jackson has double-bogeyed; you are one back of him." On the last hole, Russo's confederates told him, "If you birdie this hole you could be in a three-way tie for the lead." You can imagine how this type of traveling scoreboard could induce pressure and cause someone to lose focus on the task at hand. Bob birdied the 18th and went on to hit near-perfect shots to win on the second playoff hole.

When asked how he maintained his self-control, Russo reported that he stared at the dimples on the ball, or looked intently for scuff marks on it.

When walking between shots, Bob would look at the trees or notice how the bushes were arranged. He would strive to notice different scenery that he hadn't noticed before. The outer eye kept his mind from running wild. Vision kept him in the present and permitted him to avoid the mental gymnastics that can place winning or losing above the specific task. These techniques become an effective way to calm the mind and avoid negative thoughts. They represent aspects of visual dominance that allow you to attain peak performance. Utilize vision and the other senses to become one with the environment—to make the round a walk in the park. It beats worrying about the future or dwelling on the past.

The Dominant Eye at Address

A key factor that is seldom mentioned and often misunderstood is the correct position of the dominant eye at address. Proper eye positioning can result in less mis-hits and potentially reduce the number of three-putts, especially under pressure.

The dominant eye, as discussed in Chapter Two, is responsible for aiming correctly to the target. It is also critical to determining which head position is appropriate at address. The reason for the characteristic head turn of Jack Nicklaus, at address, is to place his dominant eye in posi-

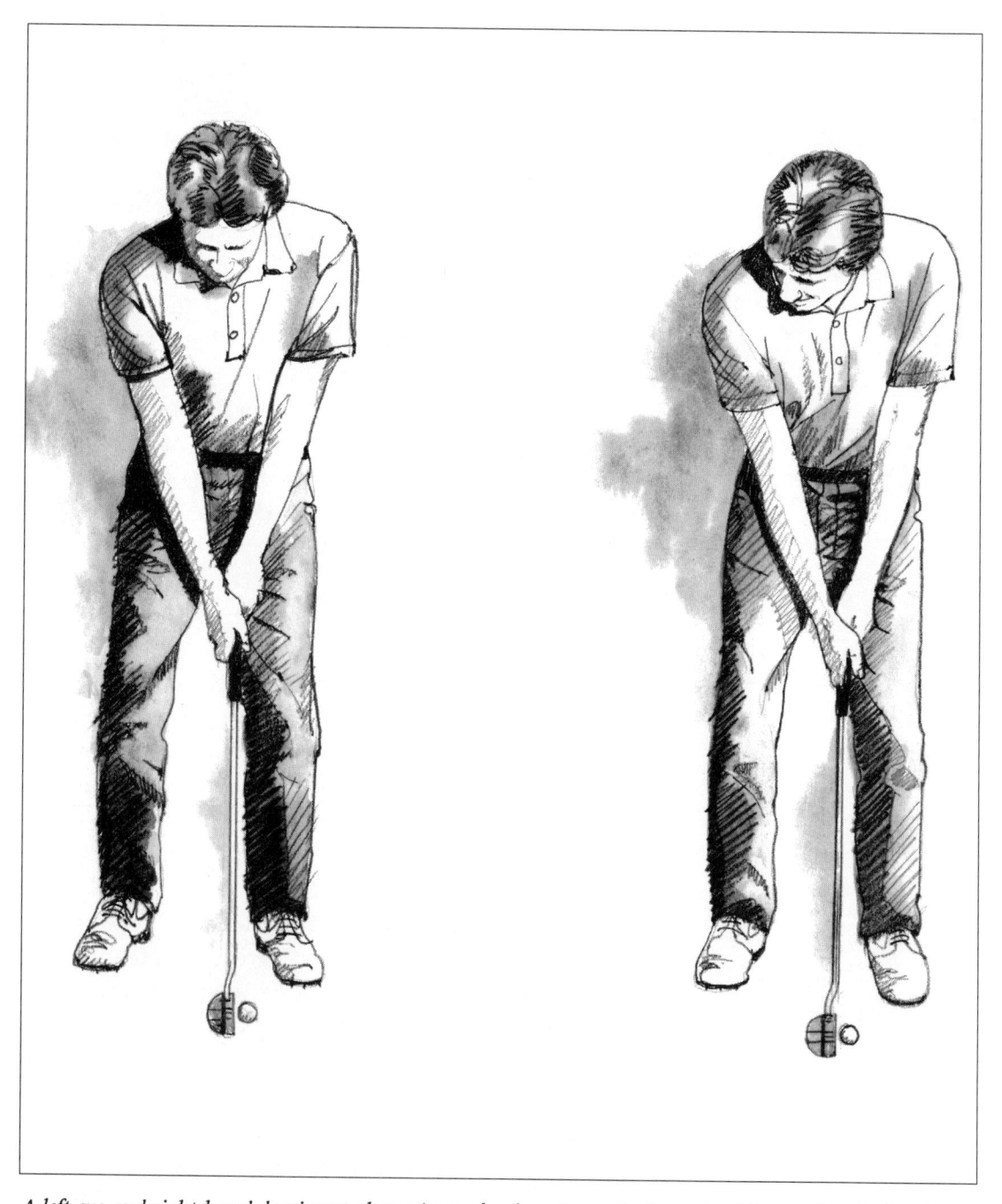

A left-eye and right-hand dominant player (cross-dominant) may be best served by rotating the head.

tion to gain a better perspective to deliver the club to the ball.

The dominant eye can affect your perception of the ball's location. Note the upper right corner of this book's relationship with an object behind it, such as a pattern on the floor or an item on the wall. Move your head just a couple of inches to the left and you will see the corner shifts perspectives to the right. If your dominant eye isn't *behind* the ball, even by a fraction of an inch, you may perceive the ball as farther toward the back foot than it really is. The eye directs the club to where it perceives the ball's location, causing the player to hit behind the ball, as the apex of the stroke is moved backward. Mispositioning the dominant eye can also affect the timing of the stroke.

Another way to appreciate the difference in perspectives is to stand over a ball at the address position. Position your hands, as recommended in Chapter Two (for finding the dominant eye), and look at the ball through the hole in your hands with your dominant eye. Now switch eyes, but leave your hands in the same position. Note the large difference in perspectives as you switch back and forth. If your dominant eye is not in the proper position, the non-dominant eye may be forced into action as the aiming eye. The result: a mistimed stroke, a mis-hit ball.

If you are right-eye dominant and address the ball as a right-handed golfer, your eye is automatically behind the ball to start, barring any unusual head tilt. If you are left-eye dominant and right-handed (cross dominant), and play from the right side, you should consider adopting a little of the Nicklaus head tilt to put your left eye behind the ball. The same recommendation applies if you are left-handed and right-eye dominant.

To properly place your dominant eye in position (if you are right-handed and left-eye dominant or left-handed and right-eye dominant), rotate your head so that it's tilted up on the side opposite the dominant eye. Turn your

head enough to place the dominant eye where the non-dominant eye was before you rotated your head. Make sure your dominant eye is not too far behind the ball. This may also result in a mistimed stroke.

Play with different head positions to see which helps you make more consistent contact with the ball. Most of all, always keep your eyes parallel to the line.

Missed Putts

During one session on the practice green at the Castle Pines course in Colorado, PGA Tour pro Kelly Gibson commented that a primary reason the pros miss the short ones is that the head moves with the eyes. Certainly, one of the most frequent comments heard after a missed putt is "you moved your head." Looking up before impact, or peeking, shows obvious goal-oriented behavior instead of sticking to the task of just hitting the ball from one point to another.

Another problem for most of us is not that we don't see clearly. We don't use our eyes to their fullest potential. Look at the light switch across the room from you. Go ahead, take a look. How far away is it in feet or yards? How many inches wide and tall is it? Once you were hit with these questions, would you look at the switch a little differently the second time? Of course.

What is disconcerting is that we so often look but do not see. Average putters often ignore details that good putters are prone to see automatically. Observing the length of a putt, the severity of slope and the direction of the grain, as well as undulations in the green will help you "see" more clearly and hole many more putts.

4

The Farnsworth System of Alignment

We act as if the little putts mean nothing, but they can tear us apart.

JOHN UPDIKE, *GOLF DIGEST*

DURING THE 1996 Masters, Nick Faldo and I agreed to see each other again when he visited Colorado for the "International." We met on the putting green. It was immediately clear to me that Nick had not stuck to his visual drills and techniques regimen I had recommended. In four months, Nick had swung from being on target with his putter to again misaligning to the target. Nick had also slipped out of the number one position on the PGA Tour's putting statistics list. He had been fussing with different equipment and concentrating on his putting stroke during practice and play, but nothing had been going as well as it had for the first part of the year.

Alignment, folks, appears to be one arena that mechanics can't remedy. From fifteen feet on, Nick was aligning to the left of the actual location of the hole. He found that countless hours of putting did not improve his alignment problems. The main reason: He was focusing on the mechanics instead of his perception.

The largest void in the how-to books on putting involves correcting alignment misperceptions. Yet, in our testing of many golfers, from the elite professional to the less skilled, we find mis-alignment to be a common problem. It is a prime reason you miss putts.

Our research points to the primary problem for alignment errors: the inability of the eyes to align the clubface to a target in the address position. This is due to the unusual perspective for the eyes having to aim while beside the ball, as golf requires, instead of behind it. In most sports, the eyes face the target. But not in golf. Golf forces us to adopt a new perspective. Everything must come from the ball as the center of the action. For alignment, the eyes must act as if they are still behind the ball even though they are physically situated beside the ball. A majority of golfers cannot accurately adjust to this perspective.

To better understand this dilemma, close your nondominant eye and point a finger at an object in the distance, such as the floor or the corner of the wall across the room. Now lean your body to the left a few inches, simulating the eyes left of the ball at address. Your finger now appears to point to the right of the dis-

Many golfers cannot adjust to golf's unique address position beside the ball. This creates a wide variety of potential mismatches of the target line.

tant object. From the port side perspective, lefties would have a tendency to align left of the hole. Maybe, now, you have a better idea of the difficult challenge for the eyes.

Your finger did not move, nor did the distant object, but the visual perspective shifted. In other words, when you move to the left of the target line, your perspective now places the target line to the right of where it was perceived when viewing from behind the finger (ball). You align according to your eyes' perspective until you learn to alter this (visual) perspective. For some, this isn't so easy. The majority of golfers need more accurate aiming clues, because vision is easily led astray.

Since Ivan Pavlov's experiments in the late 1800s, science has known that the brain's circuitry can be rewritten if it is presented with a constant stimulus. This chapter introduces proven techniques to accomplish accuracy of alignment through a constant accurate stimulus.

What would it do to a player's scoring average if he or she made 60 or 70 percent of the putts from seven feet or less? Could always seeing the line ease the anxiety of every golfer over these seemingly frightful putts? Do you always see the line? How confident are you over a four-foot putt to win the club championship?

My research shows alignment problems are caused by:

1. Improperly reading the green's characteristics.
2. The inability of the visual system to shift perspectives to appreciate even an accurate aim in the address position.
3. Not seeing the line from behind the ball, or inaccurately perceiving the target's location.
4. Utilizing a distance target, instead of a near target, to align to (or not being specific with the aim or alignment).
5. The ball's effect in creating "visual noise."

6. Improperly positioning the head and dominant eye in the address position.
7. An inaccurate ball-feet relationship at set-up.

An important key to making those critical short putts is determining the cause of your errors, then eliminating them. The above areas of concern are all visual challenges of the game of golf. If you had problems with the self-tests of "aiming accuracy" or "alignment perspective," or trouble trusting your line, then the next two chapters are designed to help you improve.

Now, let's get to improving your aim out on the golf course with the Farnsworth System of Alignment. The following is a step-by-step, sequential plan to immediately impact your alignment skills.

The Logo Alignment Aid

When Nick came to Colorado to play in the "International" at Castle Pines, five months had transpired. After watching him on the putting green briefly, it was evident that he had fallen back into old habits.

Since two of Nick's afternoons were taken up with fly fishing, one of his favorite pastimes, as well as seeing his parents, who were visiting in Colorado for the first time, I realized we needed a way to get his alignment back on track quickly. We discussed the concept of logo alignment as being a natural for him, since Nick was so good with his aiming accuracy tests.

Those who need help in appreciating the line when over the ball, and a visual guidance "tool" for aiming the putter, can use the ball's logo printed on its cover. The logo-alignment technique works so well because it helps alleviate the number one problem of those we have tested—misaligning the putter in the address position.

Using the ball's name to "aim" at the target.

Another line-up guide.

The logo alignment concept works best for those who tested better on their aiming accuracy than on their alignment perspective. The technique goes like this: The player marks his ball with a coin, determines the break, if any, then positions his ball so that the logo is "aimed" at the target while he is behind the ball. Then when addressing the ball, the player aligns the putter to the label instead of attempting to align by looking at the hole while in the address position.

Andrew Magee uses the logo for alignment on each and every putt. He determines the break, squats down behind his mark, then places the ball down so that his logo is aimed at his spot. He depends upon it so much that he admits that when he putts from off

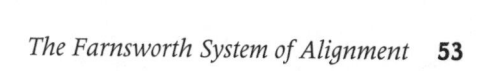

Different logo-line extensions.

A ruler can aid making a straight line.

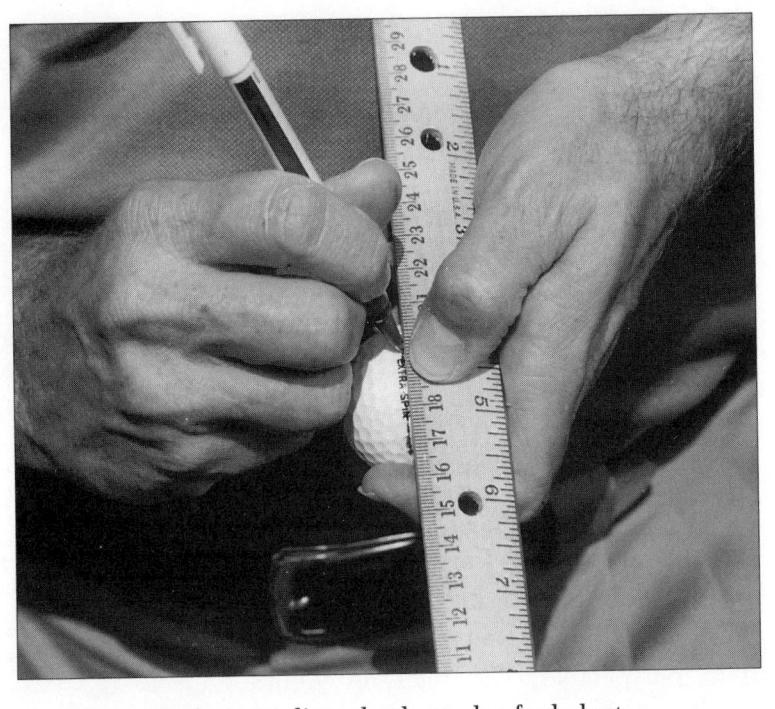

the fringe and can't align the logo, he feels lost.

Bobby Jones was reported to be the first to recommend using the logo for alignment. He must also have recognized the challenge of attempting to align when over the ball.

Some use the name *Precept,* for example, and others use the smaller *Extra Spin.* We recommend the latter because it gives a more definitive line to help in aiming.

For further help, increase the visual identification of the logo by placing a mark through the logo. Different players have found that some markings are easier to work with than others. Some prefer the line to be small. Others like the line to extend well past the name, so they can appreciate it better when standing back away from the ball. Nick marked his with small dots, because the dimple pattern did not allow any easy marking of a straight line. The bottom line: Try different ways to see which you like the most.

Keep your coin behind the ball in case you need to re-aim your logo line.

I have found that some players can better align the logo as they kneel down with their nondominant eye closed. Others have found it more accurate to keep both eyes open, while positioning their dominant eye directly behind the ball and the logo. Some have no problem placing the logo on the intended line the first time, with the two eyes bisecting the ball's logo. See which helps you get it closer the first time.

Note:

Always make sure the logo line is bisecting the ball's center as it is placed on the ground.

I have seen some players place the ball down, stand back a step or two, realize the logo is not quite exact, then adjust the aim of the putter as a compensation. This is usually done because the player felt rushed. I discourage this and favor realigning the logo. Often, it's not that time-consuming, and the players are not overusing "the clock" as much as they believe. (The player has 35 seconds from the time the previous player putts to hit his putt, once it is his turn.) I prefer the player take a step back before removing his coin and assess the aim rather than expecting to get it right the first time. Then, if necessary, he should turn the ball a dimple or two's worth toward the correct path to the target.

Some players just can't appreciate a straight (logo) line to the target, possibly because their aiming accuracy is a problem or they need a little more visual guidance. The next technique can come in handy.

Seeing the Line—Always!—with the Zorro

When you can vividly see the line of the ball's path before you putt, your level of confidence goes up. There may be

The Zorro allows a golfer to be more daring on putts.

times, as you stand behind the ball, when you can't seem to get any semblance of a putting line. If you had problems with aiming accuracy or you need help seeing the line, we propose the *Zorro.*

This technique is most valid for putts of approximately ten feet or less, but it can be used for much longer putts. It will become a powerful tool for not only seeing the line but also in obtaining an aiming point. All of my students are fascinated by a natural phenomenon of the eyes that leaves an after-image on the green, which becomes a great alignment guide.

The Zorro follows after you have determined the break. To implement this technique, stand a step or two behind the ball. Close your nondominant eye, then point your putter at the ball as if it were a sword. Position it so the ball appears to visually intersect the shaft of the putter near the handle and the hole, or the target outside the hole, intersects the shaft near the putterhead. This provides a straight line that can guide your eyes along the line they would like to see on the putting surface, but are unable to see at that time.

Next, let your dominant eye track along the shaft a couple of times at the speed of the putt you propose to hit. This helps prepare your brain and your motor system for the actual stroke to follow. It also helps activate the back of the eye (the retina) to see a special visual guidance phenomenon: The Zorro can leave an after-image on the green, not only to pick an accurate target to align to, but to mentally help your confidence by seeing the connection between the ball and the hole.

Immediately after you run your eyes up and down the shaft, remove your putter by slowly pulling your hand down to your side. When you remove the putter, you should see a dark after-image of the puttershaft on the green. The after-image is the same visual phenomenon you see when a flash bulb goes off in your face. What you are experiencing is a natural chemical reaction within

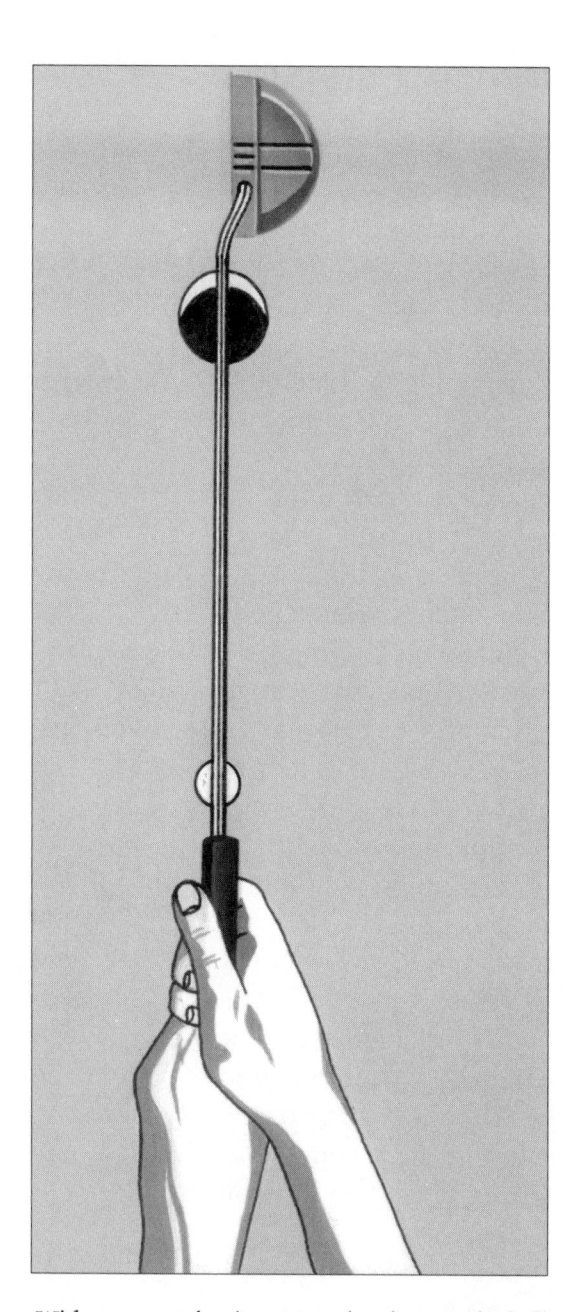

With your nondominant eye closed, cover the ball and the hole, or distance target, with the putter-shaft.

After pulling the putter down, an after-image should appear on the green.

your eyes. If you don't see it when you take the putter away, try running your eyes up and down the shaft a few more times, just looking at the shaft for a few more seconds. When trying it at home, it will help to have a plain, light carpet or floor as background.

This after-image that runs from the ball to your target will only last a couple of seconds, but it can aid your direction and your confidence as you step to the ball. The Zorro helps you when visualization of the line fails. At the very least, the Zorro helps you *see* the line. There is nothing more powerful than seeing the line.

If you have difficulty seeing the after-image, it could be from your eyes being "bleached" from the sun. This is another reason for wearing a sun shade, aside from the UV protection and the visually relaxing effect.

Even if the after-image isn't seen, you have given the brain a positive line, a connection, to the target. With time, the Zorro technique will help you trust your alignment. It can be a great visual aid to help you become like Zorro—more daring. When you are confident in your alignment, you will stroke the ball more firmly.

Aligning the logo line can be even more accurate if you take a step back or two from the ball when first aligned (leaving your coin in place). Now Zorro the line, and assess the logo's direction with the shaft. If the label is askew, you can now re-align the logo before removing your coin. After awhile, you will find you are pretty good at aligning the logo without the Zorro. Initially, however, it is a very useful tool to help you see the line's proper connection to a distance target, via the shaft.

The Learning Curve

Quite often a player says, "The lines on my putter confuse me" or "the lines don't look like I am aimed correctly."

This is because his or her visual (X-axis) perception was shifted far to the right or left of the actual location of the hole causing an accurate set-up to look askew. The real problem lies with the player now trying to assess the line while in the address position. Trust me, this is too confusing a position for most to assess the line.

I recommend that you aim the putter to the logo line, then square your stance in regard to the putter's aim. From that point on, you are not to assess the line. Move on to the next task of looking at your distant target.

When I gave the logo alignment to Tom Kite, he was aware of it, but he never felt it useful because it did not look correct to him when he stood over the ball. At address, when Tom looked down the line, he lost direction and confidence. Because of this, I recommended he avoid focusing on alignment at address. He was not allowed to assess his line when over the ball. This took time, especially with the shorter putts.

While behind the ball, Tom picked a spot a few inches in front of the ball that was on line with the intended path of the putt. He moved to the address position, first aligning his putterblade to the logo, then his feet and the rest of his body to the putterblade. After completing his alignment, he was then to look at the spot he had picked in front of the ball and to the distance target. He was allowed to look

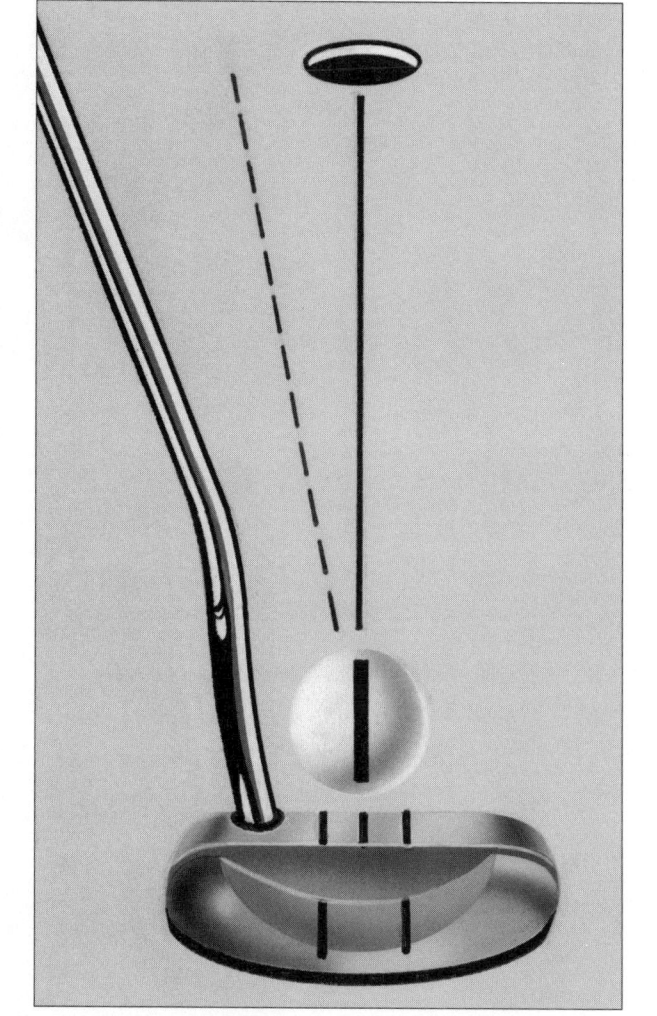

Some players swear the logo is pointing off line when they are in the address position.

Until your eyes are educated,
look only to a spot in front of
the ball and to the hole.

back at the ball only when he was ready to start his stroke.

With practice, the logo line eventually appeared to look straight to Tom. At that point, Tom's perception matched reality. Only then could he believe in his alignment. To fast-forward visual re-education of the logo concept, I recommend the following technique.

Seeing It!

At home, mark your logo as you desire on a golf ball. Start by aiming the logo at another ball located on a short weave carpet or a hardwood floor, no more than three feet away. You can use the Zorro to check it. Address the logo, aiming your putter at the logo line. Complete your address and spend time seeing what correct alignment should look like. Observe this perspective for a minute or two, then go back behind the ball and observe the direct line of the logo to the ball. Address the ball and observe this alignment perspective for another minute or two. Next, stroke the putt. Your ball should hit the target ball. If it does not, your stroke quite possibly has become a compensation for your misperception. You may, for example, be closing the putterface at impact to compensate for a right-of-the-actual-target misperception. If this is the case, you are advised to consult your local golf professional for work on a straight stroke.

When ready, use a dime for a target and repeat the above. You can also move back to six or more feet and repeat the above drill. Please realize that as you adopt this new perspective, you may still carry excessive baggage for awhile. Until your eyes and brain get in sync, they will not believe in the new perspective. Rest assured, this will go away as you work on seeing this perception. The logo alignment is too good a visual guidance tool to discard just because the eyes aren't yet re-educated.

A Common Practice

During my workshop at the 1993 Colorado PGA Academy, every pro more confidently evaluated the alignment (to a target twenty-five feet away) when positioned behind the ball than at the address position. While that may be no surprise, what is surprising is that too many attempt minor adjustments when over the ball. Some may have the visual flexibility and experience to tell if they are off line at address and are good at making those little adjustments. But most can not. Thus, my number one recommendation to players with alignment woes is: Do not re-align when over the ball. When at address, only factor the distance to the target. The line is already determined by the logo before address.

Helping with Another Potential Problem

Nick Faldo (and others) initially found it difficult to align their putters to the logo. The problem: When the putter-face looked square, it was really open. To overcome this

A "T-line" can help you aim the putter squarely.

misperception, place a T-line on the ball to align the face of the putter to, and repeat the above drill at home seeing this perspective.

Use a yardstick, at home, to square the putterface.

To further appreciate an accurate squaring of the club-face, place a yardstick on the floor and place the putter up against one end of it. Leave a half-inch or so separation between the putterface and the end of the yardstick. When the putter is square, there will be an equal distance between all points on the face and the end of the yard-stick. Place a ball on the yardstick near the end being used. Align the logo line pointing down the center of the yard-stick. When this is accomplished, spend thirty to sixty seconds appreciating what an accurate squaring to the target looks like and repeat this drill daily.

I strongly recommend for those with alignment problems to consider using a visually friendly putter: one that has at least one or more two-inch-long aim lines extending from the front to the back of the putter. If you don't prefer to change putters, have your golf professional place a line on your present putter along the sweet spot of the putter.

A visually friendly putter can help your alignment skills.

Spot Putting

Alignment of the putterface to a near target is easier for most golfers than alignment to a point much farther away. By finding a small spot along the target line and a few inches to a foot in front of the ball, the player can align more accurately. A majority of tour players use the spot putt technique.

The Zorro technique can also help in determining your spot on short putts. Remove the putter and find a distinguishing area along the after-image and near the ball, such as a small dark spot of grass. This spot allows you to align the putterface to your target as you set up.

Spot putting isn't employed by players who believe it interferes with the distance reference that helps them impart the power necessary to hit the ball into the hole. This will be

Aiming to a spot a foot in front of the ball is easier than aligning to a distance target.

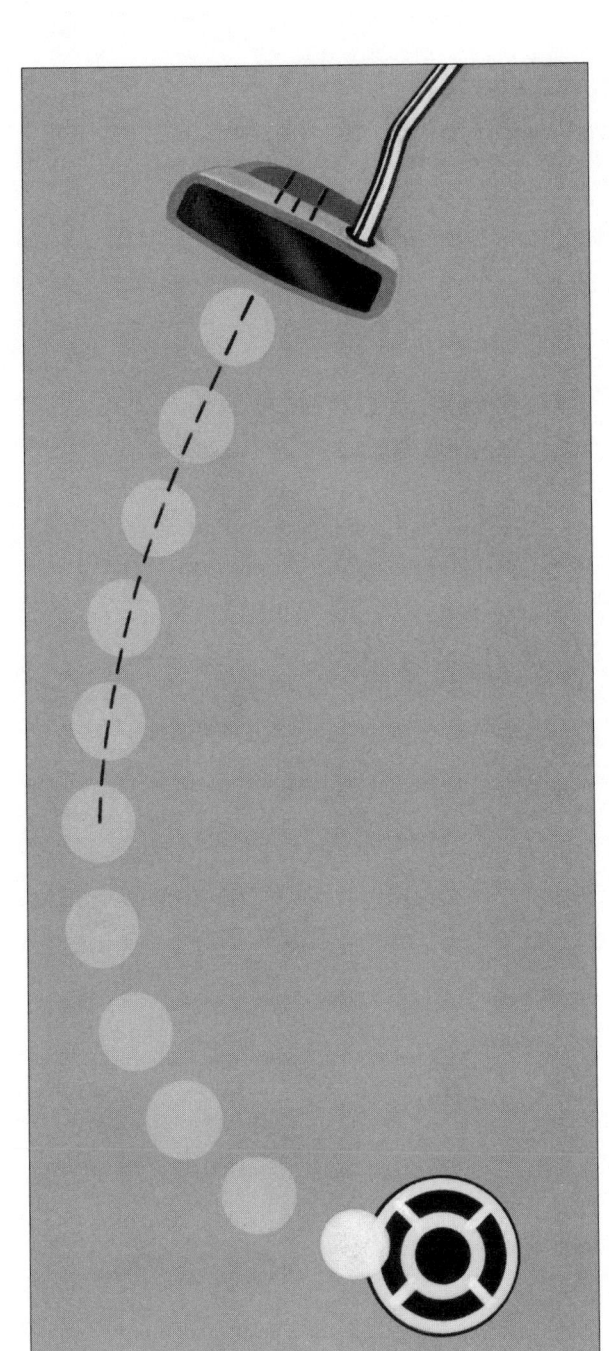

Most often the aim point is at the apex of the break.

addressed further in Chapter Eight, but for now realize that after aligning to a spot, your very next reference should be the hole, or another distance target, with no further reference to alignment. That task is already completed.

Breaking Putts

Once the break of the putt has been established, aim the logo at the spot you have chosen to be on line with the intended path. I recommended this to PGA Tour pro Hal Sutton after testing him.

I found him on the practice tee after his pro-am round. He said that he "went through thirteen holes of hell out there," until he quit using the logo on breaking putts. He felt that he needed to make the final decision when over the ball and not behind the ball. He didn't make any more putts, but he felt more comfortable when he was allowed to align his way. To me, that sounded as if Hal was not assessing the break well enough before he got to his ball, but even so, he could have left the coin there and aligned the logo when at address, then removed the coin and re-addressed the ball. Unfortunately, this would place him back to the original problem, of try-

ing to align at the address perspective, and this wasn't his strong suit. I left him to work on a more confident pre-address assessment.

As you will see in future chapters on mastering distance, the break and speed should be determined before ever aiming the logo, let alone stepping up to the ball. That way you have done your homework and are properly prepared before you address the ball.

5

More Visual Re-education with the Farnsworth System

You can get lost on the greens.

BEN CRENSHAW, ART OF PUTTING VIDEO

MOST GOLFERS ADMIT to needing to trust their line when over the ball. Aiming the ball's logo from behind the ball helps them with their alignment. Still, they seek a little further help. A technique that is identified with Nick Price, and also Steve Elkington, is placing the putter down in front of the ball before placing it behind the ball. Why does this work?

VISUAL NOISE

My research determined that a significant number of players more accurately align their putterface to a distant target without the ball's presence than when the ball comes between the putterface and their spot. The ball, for some, creates a situation that we optometrists label visual noise.

A commonly recognized example of visual noise, or interference, is when

continued

your shadow crosses the intended line of the putt. Visual noise also relates to the fact that, at address, the ball is between the putterface and your target. The ball creates a visual distraction that interferes with the eyes' appreciation of correct alignment and the line.

Nick Price counters the noise by placing the putter in front of the ball and square to his target. Next, he completes his stance. Keeping the putterface square to the line, he then places the putter behind the ball and pulls the trigger. He also adopted this technique because it gave him a better visual sense of the line.

This technique can be applied one of two ways. The first is to place the putter down behind the ball and establish your stance. Next, move the putter in front of the ball and align it to the spot you have picked with the Zorro. Pick the putter up and move it behind the ball, keeping it pointing to the same spot or line.

Some of the players I have worked with prefer to suspend their putter above the ball, so the lead edge of the putterblade aims at their spot, without the ball's interference. They then square their stance to the putterface before placing the putter behind the ball.

The Shaft

The Farnsworth System now turns to an important technique that once again gives the visual system a 'read' and an ability to see the line that will impart more confidence to the brain and the resulting motor response of the stroke. The Shaft is a four-step technique that may be your key to making it happen over that five-foot putt for the win. Some players prefer this to the logo line on shorter putts, and for their second putts instead of re-aligning the logo.

The majority of golfers I have interviewed, or had the pleasure of working with, point to the necessity of seeing the line as a must to stroke the putt with confidence. The problem: They can't trust their eyes in the alignment posi-

tion. The next technique will give you a chance to always see the line on short putts, and gain the one-upmanship you may need to make that putt for the club championship.

Position the shaft while in the address position so that the shaft covers the ball and the hole, or a distance target.

Step 1

To gain trust in alignment, you must make an accurate read of the green. You must also believe in the accuracy of your alignment. Aligning accurately can be made easy. It involves connecting the ball and the hole (or a target outside the hole) with a straight line. The putter-shaft becomes the straight line—the connection.

Step 2

Address the ball, making sure your eyes are over it. Pick up your putter and hold it parallel to the ground, so its shaft is under your eyes and far enough away to see part of the ball above and below the shaft. Position the shaft so that you see it connecting the center of the ball with the hole (or a spot left or right of the hole on breaking putts).

Look at this connection between the ball and the hole for a few seconds. Use the time to experience, to see, this connection. When you see it, you can believe it. This connection is registered in your brain and acts as a visual aid to align to the hole. The shaft becomes your on-course tie between the ball and the hole. The line it creates is what great putters see naturally. To appreciate this technique for the moment, place two balls down on the carpet, one representing the ball and the other the hole. Apply the above instructions.

With the shaft connecting the ball and hole, adjust your feet so that they are perpendicular to the shaft, or "square." When the feet are square to the line, it yields a visual guide for the stroke. Make sure you keep the shaft in place, and under your eyes, as you align your feet and body square to the shaft.

Tilting the shaft up can help for distances of five to ten feet.

It may take time to appreciate the alignment aid of the feet being square to the line, and the parallel connection between the putter and foot. The hardest adjustment can be taking the time to do this. It can appear endless and uncomfortable initially, but it should not be skipped. Making putts you may typically miss will make you more relaxed with this step.

Step 3

The third part of this technique is accomplished by tracing, or tracking, your eyes up and down the shaft a few times. An after-image will appear as a dark line (projected on the green).

If you don't see it when you take the putter away, try running your eyes up and down the shaft a few more times. Just look at the shaft for a few more seconds, or take the

shaft away by slowly pulling it down, starting with the blade end. When trying this drill at home, it will help to have a plain, light carpet as a background.

Use the shaft to square the feet. This gives you a visual guidance tool for aiming the putterface.

If the after-image is not pointing at the hole, you weren't exact on the connection of the shaft through the center of the ball or your eyes were not on line with the shaft. If this is the case, redo it or adjust your eye alignment accordingly. (The next section addresses proper eye alignment.) Some like to close their nondominant eye to better align the shaft.

Note:

For some, the after-image appears more quickly and is more visible when the puttershaft is white, because it yields more contrast than a steel or black shaft.

Step 4

While the after-image is still seen, align the putterblade to that projected line. Now you are aimed at your target, and you can stroke the putt with confidence. If done properly, alignment to the after-image guarantees accuracy of alignment to the target.

A caddie can help your green reading and alignment accuracy.

If you don't see the after-image, square your feet to the shaft as it is held, then position the putter behind the ball so that the blade is parallel to your lead foot. This "squaring" to the target acts as a visual reinforcement, giving you more confidence with your alignment.

Always attempt to practice a technique away from the course enough to make it a habit. Then you can rely on it more when taking it to the course. Too many discard a potentially valuable tip or technique because it was too distracting when playing. The course should never be an initial practice ground for something that you have to think about.

As you gain confidence in your alignment, the shaft technique may be put aside. Quite often we see players using it for only a portion of the round. After a few times, the eyes start to make an accurate connection on their own. But don't forget to bring it back if you question your alignment.

FOUR EYES ARE BETTER THAN TWO

It is always helpful to utilize another pair of eyes. Occasionally, have another person check your alignment, preferably your pro or a person you believe to be visually accurate. Several LPGA players rely on their caddies to line up almost every putt. Make sure your eyes appreciate this perspective. Don't let your "other" eyes do it all. After they align you, appreciate this new perspective. Compare it to your usual and customary position. The goal is to eventually be able to trust your eyes without a crutch. The main problem with using another's eyes out on the course is that it often places you over the ball too long, which tends to distract concentration.

Visual Positioning

In all fairness, there are no visual clues on the green for alignment. A lesson on the putting green finds you stroking the ball right at the cup because the pro has been aligning you to the target. But it isn't long before putts start to go awry when you're out on the course by yourself. A prime reason for this loss of direction can come from the eyes' inability to perceive the correct relationship of the ball's position to the feet.

An important step for some is re-educating the visual system to establish accurate "visual positioning" of the feet to the ball.

Proper positioning means that the ball is not too far forward or back in your stance. One must establish an accurate and consistent positioning relationship: between the ball and the lead foot, the eyes, body, feet and the putter. If not, alignment problems are imminent.

The best ball position depends upon where your putter "bottoms out" during the stroke, or where it should when you are in a proper position with your stance and hand

A proper ball position tends to keep the player on line with the target.

position at address. This should be somewhere between the lead foot and the middle of your stance. To tackle this problem, call your golf professional for a putting lesson.

Note:

Before the lesson, please refer to the recommendations in Chapter Two, under the section Seeing Through the Eyes of a Champion.

Bring a large sheet of paper to the lesson. I recommend a 27x32-inch sheet from your local business or art store. Have your pro trace the outline of the ball at the top edge of the paper and the outline of your feet (as you stand in the proper address position) on the opposite edge of the paper.

I encourage you, at least for now, to square everything, including the feet. Why? Because your eyes will have more support. I am not questioning the pros who say an open stance helps them see the line more clearly. Granted, seeing the line helps you stroke the putt with more confidence, because you are more visually directed. But for those with alignment problems, I greatly discourage an open stance for now. The eyes need direction, so set your feet square to the target line.

At home, get into your putting stance on the paper and pay attention to how this looks. Observe this relationship, every day, for a minute or so. Let your eyes take it all in. How far are the feet from the ball? Make sure you know the exact distance. (Yes, this means using a ruler). How far apart are the feet? Also know this measurement: How far is the lead foot in front of the ball? I strongly recommend you use an actual ball on the circle. Keep working to see an accurate positioning relationship, and soon you will trust yourself—and your stroke—on the course.

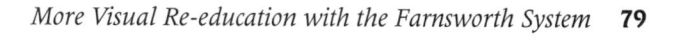

Marking an accurate ball position for home drills.

Note:

After you are concrete in your visual perception of proper positioning you can adopt an open stance.

Eyes on Line

Once you have established a square clubface and an accurate visual positioning, it is imperative that your eyes are on line and square to the line. If not, great alterations in your perception can occur.

The importance of correct eye positioning, directly above the intended line, cannot be stressed enough. If the eyes are beyond the line, perception will be shifted to the left of the intended path, thereby causing you to misalign to the left of the hole. If the eyes are inside the line, perception will be shifted to the right of actual, thereby causing you to align to the right.

Proper eye positioning may be all that is needed to render an accurate perception at address. If you were off line on the dot-to-dot test, but only on occasion when putting, checking your eye position to make sure they are on line is a good idea. Feel free to repeat the dot-to-dot test, but this time make sure your eyes are directly above the intended path.

With the eyes over the ball, they are in a better position to direct the stroke and avoid heel or toe mis-hits. If the eyes are beyond the ball, the ball is often hit with the heel of the putter. The reason for this is that the eye is anchoring the stroke from a position that aims the putter's heel toward the ball. This perspective also results in a tendency to hit the ball left of the target.

Golfers who have their eyes too far inside the ball tend to hit more putts on the toe. That's because they move

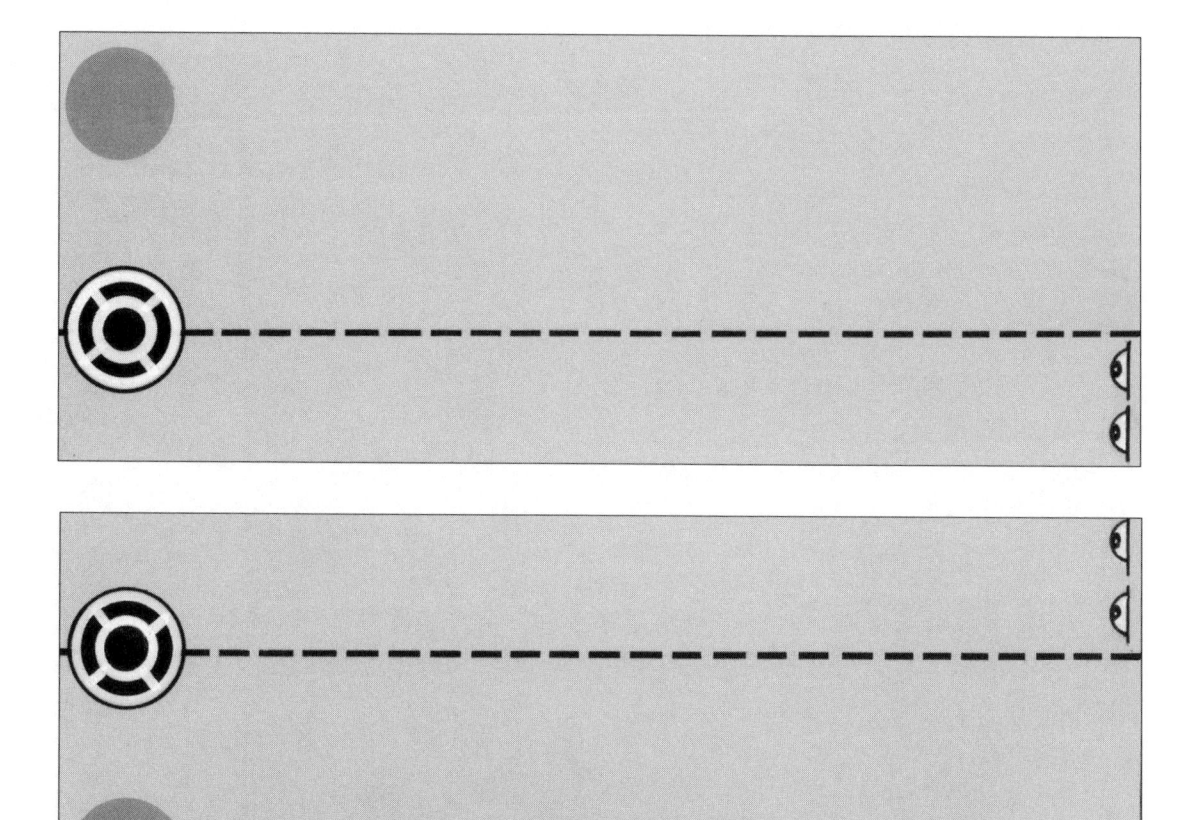

their anchor, and aiming point of the clubface, inside the line. This perspective results in the ball being hit to the right of the target line. A toed or heeled putt will not have the force to arrive at the hole.

Eyes positioned inside the line (top) cause the perception of the hole to be shifted to the right of its actual location.

Eyes positioned outside the line (bottom) shift the hole, perceptually, to the left of its actual location.

YOUR FIRST TASK ON THE PUTTING GREEN

Before any round, it would be ideal to utilize an aiming accuracy drill. I recommend our players do this drill before going to the practice tee. This drill approximates the putting-to-a-coin drill in Chapter Three. Find a level spot on the putting green and place four coins down; a dime in front and three pennies one foot behind it.

Stand three feet away from the dime and align the logo line to the dime. Check it with the Zorro if need be. Your intent is now to align your putter to the logo and stroke the ball over the dime so that it does not go farther than the pennies behind the dime. This gives you practice at aiming accuracy, and it gives you stroke control.

The object is to hit the dime three times in a row without rolling the ball past the pennies. When this is accomplished, you now graduate to the six-foot range and repeat the drill.

This drill gives you even more valuable insight and a chance to rectify any mechanical problems. If your alignment is good but you miss left of the coin, for example, you are either closing

The coin drill is a must for opening practice.

your blade at impact or cutting your stroke.

This is a great way to start the day fine-tuning your eyes and your stroke.

OTHER ALIGNMENT AIDS

Peripheral vision plays a major role in putting, because the periphery of the retina is largely responsible for referencing where you are in relation to a distance target. By standing tall instead of crouching down at address, your peripheral vision has a better chance to be used.

continued

An upright stance accents peripheral vision. . .

while a crouched stance decreases the peripheral.

Your ability to orient yourself in relation to a target is also the responsibility of the muscles in the back near the neck. It is important these muscles are relaxed and of equal tonus. I recommend an occasional massage.

Putters that are designed to compensate for your visual errors of alignment are now being promoted as a cure-all. These devices can be helpful if used properly to compensate for misperceptions. Obviously, compensation is a quick fix, and one would best be advised to work on overcoming any inherent visual misperceptions.

Summary

1. After determining to the best of your ability whether any break exists, aim the logo on the ball at the highest point of the break.
2. Use the Zorro to see the intended line.
3. Run your eyes along the shaft of the putter, or along the ground, as if they were following a conveyor belt.
4. Pick out a spot on the green along the edge of the puttershaft or on the after-image left by the puttershaft.
5. Adjust the ball's logo alignment to the spot if necessary.
6. Aim the putterface at the spot, or at the logo line.
7. If you find the ball creates visual noise, align the putterface in front of the ball, or on top of the ball, before you place it behind the ball.
8. Make sure your dominant eye is in the correct position.
9. If you don't trust your line, use the Shaft technique.
10. If all else fails, use your caddie for a second pair of eyes.

6

Mastering the Distance Challenge with the Inner Eye

The will to win is important. The will to prepare is vital.

JOE PATERNO

USE OF THE inner eye is too valuable a tool to be given short shrift. Since most putts you encounter on the golf course will be breaking putts and often are a moderate to long distance, the use of visualization allows to better judge your aim point and to better assess the energy for the stroke in order to get the ball to the hole at the correct speed.

One of the reasons for wasted strokes is a breakdown in delivering the right pace to the ball on medium-range and long-range putts. This inability leaves players with long second putts. On some putts, it may seem like the distance from ball to hole is from one area code to another. But the ability to score consistently, whether for a low or a high handicapper, most often comes down to getting the ball close to the hole from almost any place on the green.

When faced with a long putt of fifty feet or more, many golfers respond with an analysis that goes something like

A long putt should not create a negative mind-set.

this, "Wow, what a long putt." Sometimes it is more like, "Here comes a three-putt for sure."

Possibly the greatest obstacle to good performance is a negative mind-set. Because it involves our strongest sense, mental attitude is a powerful opponent. Likewise, because it often means that the subconscious mind has overpow-

ered the conscious mind, you can start thinking negatively in the middle of the putting stroke. Because it incorporates the visual, a negative attitude, or a negative visualization, is the putter's *public enemy number one.*

A perfect example of coming under the power of the negative can start when you say to yourself, "Don't three-putt." Words help create a negative image that is difficult to overcome. On the green, one three-putt begets another. Soon the negatives take over and you find yourself saying "Don't three-putt again." Or "If I three-putt this hole, I'm finished." It doesn't take much to totally lose your confidence.

A negative visualizer also has related traits to watch out for. They tend toward defensiveness, self-criticism, resentment, suspicion, fear, and worry. Such thoughts can be, and often are, self-destructive. They steal away from the positive energy you need to come to grips with the environment.

You act according to the images you hold in your mind. Research has shown negative visualization activates different muscle firing than positive visualization. Negative images can cause a hurried, uncoordinated stroke that doesn't come close to resembling that smooth, confident one you exhibited on the practice green. Negative visualization creates a negative flow of energy. When people are overcome with negative images their muscles feel devoid or zapped of power. They stand over a three-foot putt, fearful of missing the hole.

People who are prone to focus on the negative and always expect the worst, often get what they picture. They are subconsciously arranging conditions toward failure.

Most of those who acquire the "yips"—a malady of nerves—appear to be the analytical kind. They can analyze with the best of them, but this strength can turn into a weakness. As Gary McCord said in his popular book, *Golf for Dummies,* "putting could be so much fun if I didn't have

a brain." I also believe that when this malady occurs, the player has allowed negatives to permeate his or her thinking.

Let's face it, no one has ever made them all. But when one focuses on the misses instead of the makes, or tends toward negative versus positive thinking, then the mind starts to see or expect misses. This is all the more reason to end each putt, or each session on the course, with the mental discipline of seeing the positive.

The trick becomes to find a way to stay positive, or at least decrease the negative images. Let's start on the positive.

Will, Imagination, and the Positive

There is a saying in hypnosis, "When will and imagination get together, imagination always wins." No matter how much you will it to happen, if you imagine the opposite, the visual images are more likely to win out. This brings us to a supreme point. Positive thinking may not be enough to counteract negative visualization. You must exercise the power of visualization and imagination rather than try to will it.

Positive thinking does have benefits, but only when it matches the images you hold in your mind. If you think "I am going to putt this golf ball into the hole" while imagining (visualizing) another missed putt to the left, I promise you the results will not be as positive as you *think*.

In other words, it is nearly impossible to think positive and hold a negative image and experience good results. We see many golfers with all the talent in the world who do not see themselves there yet. They need to make a commitment to always see the positive.

Once your visualizations are consistently positive, you will increase your success. A good starting place is when the golfer looks at himself in the morning and sees suc-

cess. It is paramount that you focus on positive images of what to do before the stroke and reflect on the positives of each round.

Nothing yields confidence like success. But confidence may be quite elusive if you have just missed two makeable putts in a row. Don't wait for success to be the determinant of confidence. Golf doesn't work like that. There are too many chances for failure.

Positive visualization can, and must, always start any action in order for you to have a chance to be successful. Even correct mechanics tend not to be fruitful without a positive stimulus.

Correct muscle tension and control is largely dependent upon your ability to vividly channel the appropriate energy to the muscles through positive visualization. You must always work toward seeing the positive to keep your systems from going haywire and destroying the timing for the task.

Maintain a positive approach after a round. Typically, the 19th hole is filled with self-bashing over missed putts. It is a lot more beneficial to call upon positive experiences. Make sure you discuss (at least to yourself) the positives of your round and what went right on some of the greens. Always retrieve a positive experience—even after a bad putting round.

It is important to understand the difference between telling yourself (thinking positive) to do something and picturing it happening. It is equally important to appreciate the difference between instructing oneself to hit the ball at a positive target versus telling oneself where not to hit the ball. By telling oneself not to hit the ball toward the lake or not to hit it out of bounds on this hole, the mind has a last stimulus that is of a negative situation—the lake or out of bounds. The motor system is more easily directed toward what is registered, especially if there is a picture of the lake, for example, in the brain. It shouldn't be a source

of amazement if the ball goes right toward the area you just pictured or told yourself not to do. The opposite can occur from a fear of what not to do, which results in the player hitting the ball so far in the other direction that the chance of a par is equally a challenge.

Always leave the brain with a what-to-do versus what-not-to-do. Direct your eyes toward a positive target. Leave the brain with a positive visual picture. See a specific target and let that be what the brain registers as you start your swing.

On the green, it becomes an avoidance of the negative such as "don't three-putt, you idiot," to seeing the putt necessary with your *inner* eye and having a positive target to hit to.

Along the same vein, a player should not dismiss negative putts and move on. The player has seen a negative (image) occur, and the mind has registered it. If you are the kind of player who tends to remember the fat shot as you take your stance for the next shot and could well hit it thin, then you tend to overuse that negative image.

Every player should have a time to deal with negative images. This should be done when the player has time to sit down and revisit the last round, two or three. It is imperative that the player gives the positive a chance. Every putt that was not hit to perfection should be imagined being hit properly. Every putt should be revisited as if it were a real putt, with checkpoints of eyes over the ball and so forth—go through your routine. The player should see the putt travel on the correct line and with the correct speed and fall into the hole.

Always Leave with a Positive

Keep a diary. Following every round, write down what went right and why you felt it did. Fill the diary with only positive experiences.

Positive pictures result in a proper channeling of your energy and emotions. When your performance falls off under pressure, first check whether you used visualization to see a positive result before the action. To start any performance, see it happen in a positive way. Use your imagination to a positive end, like all great putters do.

A KEY TO GREATNESS

In a December 1993 *GOLF Magazine* article, Jack Nicklaus discussed what makes him tick. The game's greatest player has always been recognized as an exceptional pressure putter.

Nicklaus said, "I never hit a shot, even in practice, without having a very sharp, in-focus picture of it in my head." Nicklaus' visualization skill is still probably his greatest weapon. He knows that underlying every great achievement is the performance skill of visualization—the inner eye.

A VISUALIZATION TIP

During the Warren Smith Invitational at Cherry Hills Country Club, I noticed that my playing partner and host, golf professional Russ Dawson, never looked at the ball when he putted. He always looked in front of it, where he wanted his putter to go. This is another unique visual guidance tip that can aid those of you who tend to freeze over the ball, think negatively, and either decelerate their putter or stop it abruptly at impact. This is usually brought on by the mentality that the task is just to hit the ball, instead of to hit the ball from Target A (the ball) to Target B (the distance target).

continued

Those with the "just hit the ball" mentality usually find their ball stopping short of the hole. Russ found that the technique of looking ahead of the ball took his mind off the ball (and off making or missing) and helped him employ a positive stroke that propelled the ball toward the target.

I like the method because it has such a positive ring to it—take the club to where you are looking. How simple! For some, this technique will take practice. Try it at home. Don't be afraid of techniques. Remember, the ball is stationary. It isn't going to move until you hit it.

Using a different fixation point other than the hole can help you stroke through the ball.

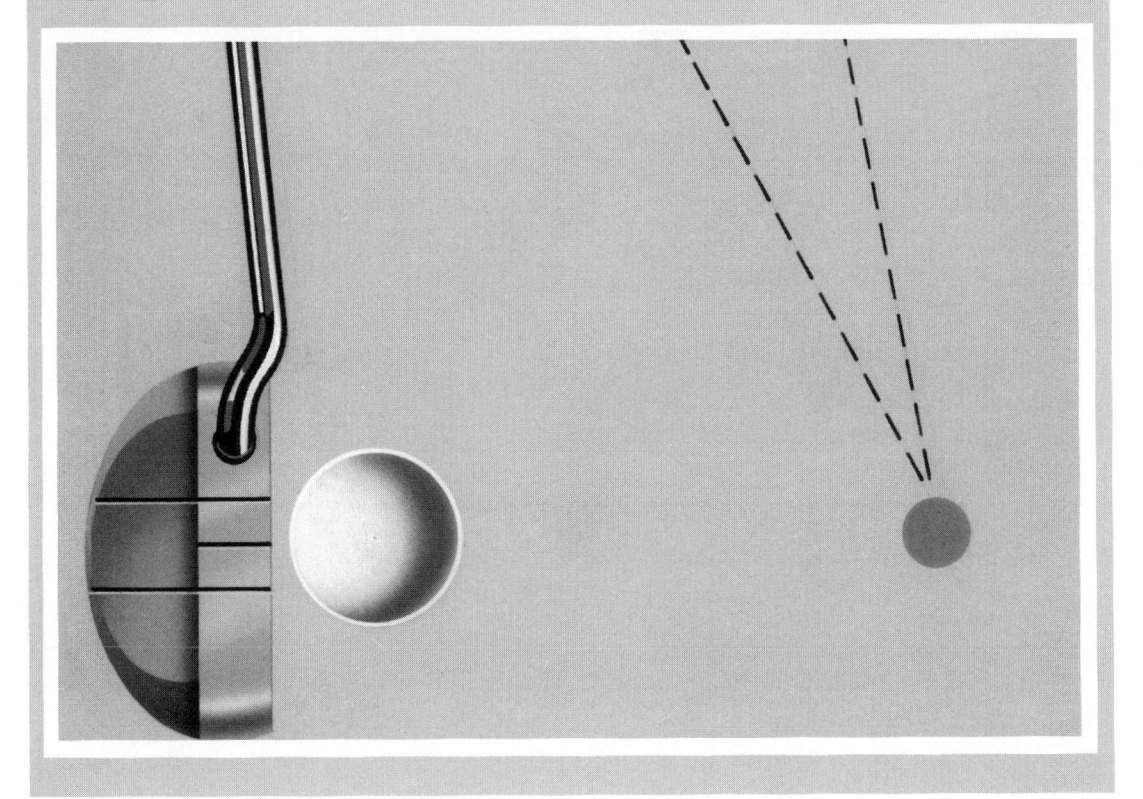

Note:

After Brad Faxon won the 1997 Freeport-McDermott classic, he was quoted, "I've always been a good putter. It is what I practice least. I'm a big believer that you have to use all your time believing you're a good putter."

Since I have tested Brad and given his eyes' perception a "Best I Have Ever Tested" award, it is clear that practice putting is only a tune-up for him. But his comments of spending time on the mental cannot be overstated or overdone.

Summary

In summary, the proper use of the inner eye can be an important key to reaching that next level. However, to further promote a positive putting attitude:

1. Start each day with a session of seeing yourself make putts that weren't made the day before, or making putts on greens you are to play today. Face each stroke with a belief that the task at hand is a masterable challenge.
2. See yourself read the break and grain, so you're sure of where to aim and how hard to stroke the putt.
3. See yourself make a focused, technically sound practice stroke before you putt. Don't just wave the putter back and through.
4. Walk up to the ball with a confident attitude. See the putt drop into the hole before triggering the stroke.
5. Make a diary. Fill in what went right and what will go right tomorrow.

7

Getting It Close—Always!— with the Inner Eye

Quite probably, everyone has experienced visualization failing them at one time or another.

PAUL RUNYAN, PGA HALL OF FAME

THE CALLER WAS an interpreter, representing TV Asahi, out of Tokyo. He politely asked if they could bring Isao Aoki to my office, "*tomorrow!*" I thought, what am I to offer one of golf's acknowledged elite putters? What I discovered, and the technique to follow, had a major impact on Mr. Aoki's ability to master the long putt and set a personal best, four-week prize-winning streak.

This chapter will address the continued use of the inner eye to avoid three-putts. First, let's take a look at a master of the inner eye. He represented the modern-day David versus Goliath. Meet Paul Runyan.

In the 1938 PGA Championship at Shawnee Country Club in Pennsylvania, Paul Runyan, at five feet seven inches, weighing all of 132 pounds, overcame a disadvantage of forty yards off the tee to beat Sam Snead, 8 & 7, when the PGA was match play. Runyan did it with his short game. And it continued to be a marvelous advantage

into later life. When he was in his late sixties, I witnessed his victory in a Colorado PGA pro-am tourney in which he used a wood for his second shot to many of the par–4s on the rain-soaked Lakewood Country Club. His PGA Championship, along with his other twenty-seven Tour victories, were tributes to his supreme visualization skills.

As his eye doctor and occasional golf companion, I can remember chasing Runyan as he almost ran from shot to shot at the Green Gables Country Club in Lakewood, Colorado. If you could keep up with him, he would share some marvelous stories of his early years on the golf circuit. There was no shot he couldn't hit, especially around the green. Using visualization, he would see in his mind's eye what type of swing was necessary to get the ball near the hole. Most of all, he could putt! If he missed a fifteen-footer during a noncompetitive round, he'd stop the action and putt from the same spot until he made it. That never took very long.

Runyan was convinced that the eyes were largely responsible for his success. He would constantly prod me to apply vision to golf at a different level than had been espoused previously. Runyan was a marvelous teacher, yet much practice with Runyan's help didn't get me anywhere near his perfection around the green. Something more basic was missing. It was much later before I understood the concept of accuracy of visualization.

Let's test your visualization accuracy. Look at the "path" below. When ready, place your pen or pencil at Start. Then close your eyes and trace down the middle of the path, keeping your pen on the paper. When you believe you are at Finish, open your eyes and check your accuracy. *Do not practice tracing with your pen or hand before you start.*

Isao Aoki, after falling woefully short of reaching the finish of the path, asked to repeat it. He reached the same result. I suggested that, instead of just looking at the path

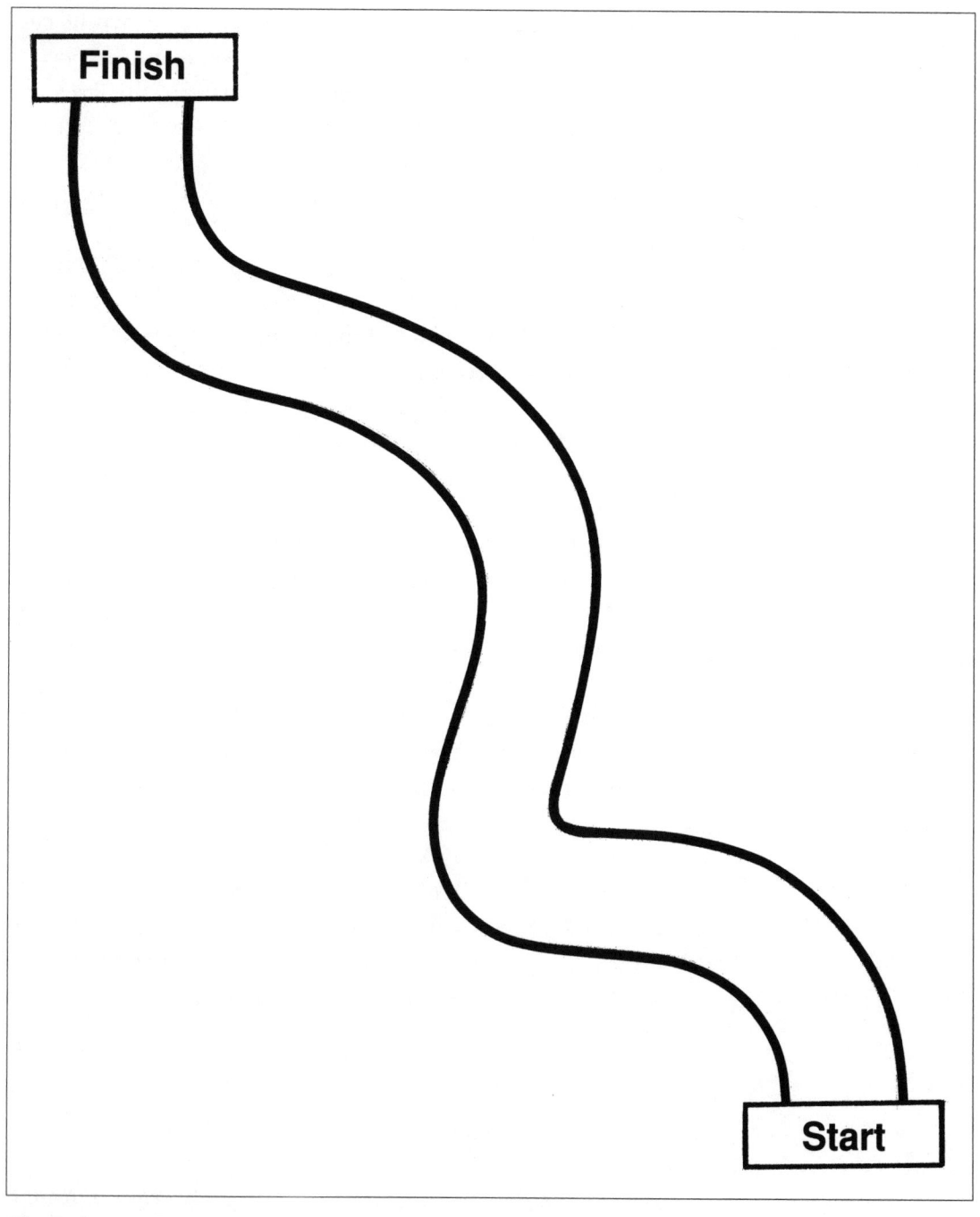

The Path.

before he started "drawing," he run his eyes down its center a couple of times, at the speed he would expect to trace it while, too, experiencing the length of the lines, the angles and so on. After complying with these recommendations, he traced the path so accurately that he couldn't have done it better with his eyes open. Mr. Aoki is a great visualizer. He just needed to apply his skill.

If you were inaccurate on The Path, it may be because you did not trace it with your eyes before using a pencil. If so, you may only need to practice using visualization *before* attempting a task. By all means, a poor showing on this test does not mean one cannot use visualization effectively. If you did trace it with your eyes and were still inaccurate, then improving the accuracy of your visualization may greatly help the usefulness of your inner eye skills.

Most of the time we do not give visualization a chance. Take a moment to reflect upon the last time you were faced with a putt of between twenty and thirty feet. Imagine the ball from the moment it leaves the blade until it stops. Now, be honest. Did you see the ball all the way? Did your recollection appear vivid or sketchy?

Imagine you have an extremely fast, twenty-five-foot downhill putt. Can you see its speed as it rolls all the way, or is it difficult to imagine the entire roll? Repeat this exercise for a thirty-foot uphill putt. Can you see the different speeds the ball goes through before it stops? If you are vivid in your picturing the above exercises, you are probably a competent visualizer. All you may need is a reminder to use visualization properly before each and every putt. And here is how.

The Technique

Despite his unusual putting style, Mr. Aoki was accurate in his alignment to a target at fifteen feet. He let me know

quickly that he was leaving moderate to long putts short of the hole. This was no surprise, based on his initial Path exercise results. He let me know, too, that before he putted he would look at the hole, from behind the ball, to "feel" the distance. I thought, "No wonder he's got a problem."

Feeling distance is not enough. To properly prepare before each putt, *the inner eye must always visualize the ball traveling over the intended path at the necessary speed, and falling into the hole.* Pre-putt visualization, if accurate, becomes a positive flow of energy, a guide for the muscles of action.

Estimate how far you are from the farthest point in the room you presently occupy. Did you notice your eyes "walking" the distance as they traversed to the point? If they didn't, they should have. By moving your eyes through space, you can better appreciate distance through the time your eyes take to get from one point to another. You didn't feel the distance—you *saw* it. If you just look at a distant point and "eyeball it," you can be fooled. The first point of business is to always walk off each putt. Don't guesstimate. Walk it. Know your distance.

The majority of golfers I have worked with tend to look at the distance point for information, but do little to appreciate the speed necessary to get the ball to the hole. Very few can just eye the putt, get a feel and obtain accurate results. The rest need a better tool to appreciate the space between themselves and the distance target. Most need to strive for accuracy of visualization to properly prepare the mind and the body for the action.

Imagine watching Tiger Woods hit a drive. Attempting to see the ball's incredible speed, in the first few yards, you can appreciate the energy generated. Imagine the energy generated by seeing yourself toss a golf ball over your house. Now imagine the energy necessary to putt to a hole five feet away. There is a tremendous difference in the energy necessary for the drive compared to the five-foot putt.

*Don't guesstimate
your distance,
always walk it off.*

There was also a difference in your eye speed as you projected the ball's speed in the aforesaid examples. Could you experience the body's muscles "loading" for the impending toss as you imagined throwing the ball over the house? What you have just experienced is part of the preparatory phase, initiated by a visual picture.

When you visualize in real-time, your eye muscles move as they imagine an object moving, say from left to right across the visual field. The eye muscles also are activated when you visualize a ball rolling along the green. Technically, this causes a sequenced firing of retinal cells, which sends an electrical signal to the cortex of the brain that, in turn, imparts a signal to the motor (muscle) system. A significant percentage of the retinal fibers go to the cortex for translation into motor functioning. The speed at which the eye muscles diverge as the brain imagines the ball speeding away from the impact point keys the muscles involved in putting. The more accurately the visualization fits the situation, the more likely the results will be the same.

Visualization Applied

The pre-putt visualization technique goes as follows: See yourself standing or kneeling a few feet behind the ball, facing the hole, with your eyes looking at the ball. Now make your eyes feel as if they are *pushing* the ball toward the hole.

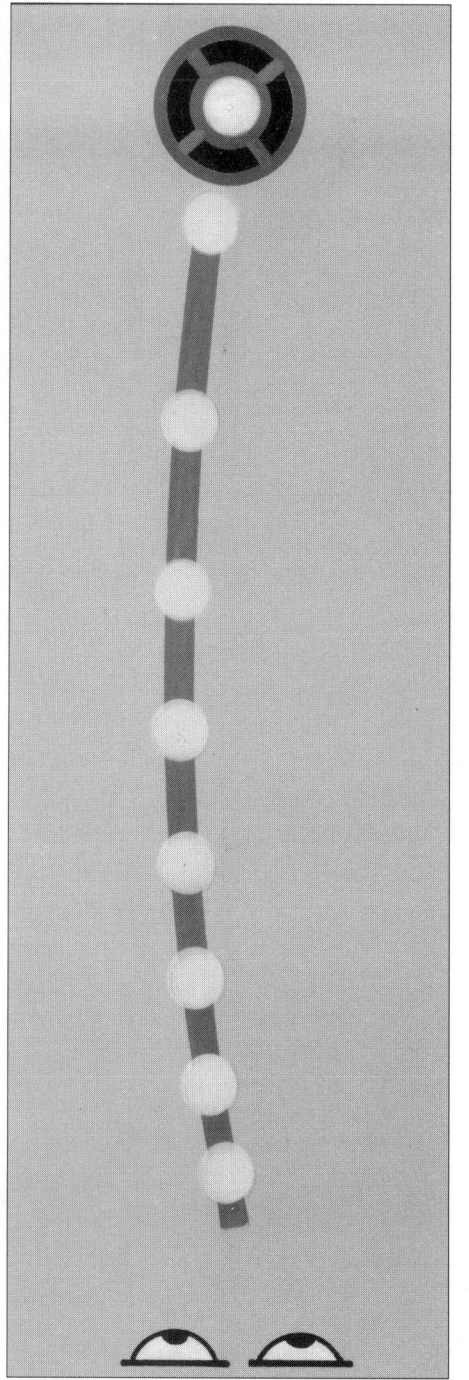

By seeing the ball's intended roll, the brain is provided with a positive image—and the motor system, with a precise energy stimulus for action.

Pushing renders a more positive transfer from the eyes to the motor system than if the eyes just moved along the green without a purpose. The different speeds or phases of divergence of the eye muscles, as they move farther out in space, form the basis of this preparatory phase. The speed of the eyes supplies the body's muscles with the energy needed for the action. This energizing of the muscles is what the visual-motor has the power to do. You can get a feel by looking at a far target, but I emphatically state it isn't as accurate a stimulus as *seeing the ball's speed with the mind's eye*. Through practice, you will discover that this will transfer more effectively to the motor system than feel will.

I told Mr. Aoki that by using this inner eye technique before each putt, he would more accurately prepare his muscles for the stroke. This technique would help him better appreciate the distance, provided he "watched" the ball travel all the way to the hole before he putted. He left promising to start using his eyes more to his advantage on the green.

As a sidelight, Mr. Aoki won his next two tournaments, his first and second ever on the Senior Tour. He finished in the top ten in the next tournament and lost in a playoff the following week—giving him a personal PGA four-tourney record of over $300,000.

To just look at the distance and feel it isn't using your visual powers to the fullest. Precede every stroke with a visualization of the speed of the ball—from the time it is struck to the time it rolls into the hole. If nothing else, this allows you to stroke the putt with confidence.

During putting clinics, I have seen that the visualization technique has been the most difficult to impart. Few can visualize the ball rolling along the green, putt after putt. For this technique to be learned, it must be practiced over and over. Furthermore, if you are under stress, you will have a problem.

When Visualization Fails

You must have a preparation phase—a pre-shot component—so vision can direct your body's muscles. One such tool comes from a unique concept I call *in-vision-ing*. In-vision-ing refers to the use of the eyes' visual-motor system to track along the ground at the pace the ball must travel to arrive at the hole at the correct speed.

Visualization requires a self-directed image of the ball. In-vision-ing asks you to move your eyes' line of sight along the ground at the speed necessary without having to self-generate an image of the ball. Herein lies the vital difference that separates visualization from in-vision-ing. The cortex receives the information in much the same way with in-vision-ing as visualization-through a visual stimulus.

Can we get these tiny eye muscles, weighing a few ounces, to direct the action of the large muscle groups used for putting without calling upon visualization? Emphatically the answer is "Yes!"

The technique of in-vision-ing also furnishes a stimulus for action that ends up loading energy into the muscles. This loading will be a reference for the action to follow. This visual-motor action is effective whether the person visualized the ball rolling or used in-vision-ing. As you perfect this technique, you will master the accuracy of the visual-motor to match what is necessary for the situation. When the eye muscles are allowed to lead the action, and when the motor begins to trust the eyes and coordinate with them, this technique will show powerful results.

In order for in-vision-ing to be effective, the pace of the eye muscles must be accurate. The following techniques are important for those who find visualization or in-vision-ing difficult to employ. They aid your accuracy of visualization through awareness and fine-tuning of this valuable skill.

Real-Time

In my clinics I was originally so foolish as to believe that announcing the technique of running the eyes along the green before the putt would be a major breakthrough in performance for all. A missing element was a more accurate perception of the ball's roll.

Question: How long will it take for the ball to roll, from impact to the hole, on a level forty-foot putt on your course under regular conditions? Will it take five seconds? Six seconds? As many as ten or twelve seconds? Would it take more or less time for an uphill forty footer? How about a forty-foot downhiller?

Real-time refers to the total time a putt would take from the moment it is hit to when it stops. Real-time can be an important key to putting consistency by way of visualization accuracy. At the very least, real-time can add more specifics to your pre-putt visualization, and to your muscles, regarding the action to follow.

Answer: A putt of forty feet will take around 5.8 to 6.2 seconds on a level part of a green. For a forty-foot putt that is uphill, it would take 4.7 to 5.1 seconds. Thus, an uphill putt takes less time to travel than does a level putt of the same length.

Don't be upset if your answers to the opening questions were incorrect. Not one of my students, including a U.S. Women's Amateur champion and a Colorado State High School champion, were right either. All thought the uphill putt either took more time or the same amount of time as a level putt of the same distance.

The reason the uphill putt takes less time is two-fold. First, the speed of the initial phase of the uphiller must be faster paced to compensate for gravity. Second, when the ball gets closer to the hole, gravity slows it down more quickly than if it were level. Fast deceleration creates shorter elapsed time than slower deceleration.

On a putt of the same distance that is downhill, the ball will roll for over seven seconds. Why? Because it needs to be slower paced in its initial phase, and because, in its final phase, it will decelerate more slowly and longer, due to gravity's tendency to pull it down the slope.

So what's the big deal? What difference does a second make? Basically, the difference between success and failure. Let's look at real-time tables for three courses to appreciate differences and similarities. The following are ranges of time for three putts at each of the distances listed.

	ARROWHEAD	CHAMPIONS (HOUSTON)	CHERRY HILLS
Distance (in feet)		*Time (in seconds)*	
LEVEL PUTT			
10	3.0–3.2	2.7–2.9	3.2–3.3
20	4.1–4.2	4.1–4.2	4.5–4.6
30	5.1–5.2	5.0–5.2	5.2–5.5
40	5.8–6.2	6.0–6.2	6.2–6.3
MILD UPHILL PUTT			
10	2.5–2.8	2.4–2.6	2.5–2.7
20	2.9–3.2	3.5–3.7	3.4–3.6
30	3.8–4.3	3.9–4.0	3.9–4.2
40	4.7–5.1	4.5–4.8	4.6–4.9
MILD DOWNHILL PUTT			
10	4.5–4.8	3.8–4.1	4.3–4.6
20	5.0–5.2	5.0–5.2	5.1–5.3
30	6.4–6.5	6.0–6.4	6.2–6.5
40	7.1–7.3	7.4–7.8	7.3–7.7

Real-time can vary from course to course and condition to condition, including the degree of the slope and the type, length and direction of the grain. By appreciating real-time,

we are more specific and complete with visualization or in-vision-ing. We run less of a chance of short-cutting this crucial skill. Real-time asks you to run your eyes across the green at the same speed and time as the conditions (distance, slope and grain) demand. So the forty-foot level putt should take you six seconds to in-vision.

Phases of Speed

Mastering accuracy of visualization also entails an understanding of the different speeds the ball incurs on its way to the hole. In most situations, the ball speed undergoes three phases:

1. Acceleration.
2. Neutral.
3. Deceleration.

ACCELERATION

Deceleration, Neutral, and Acceleration phases represent different ball speeds.

The Acceleration phase starts as the ball is struck, but can occur on a downhill putt whenever the ball encounters a steep grade. This phase (for level or uphill putts) encom-

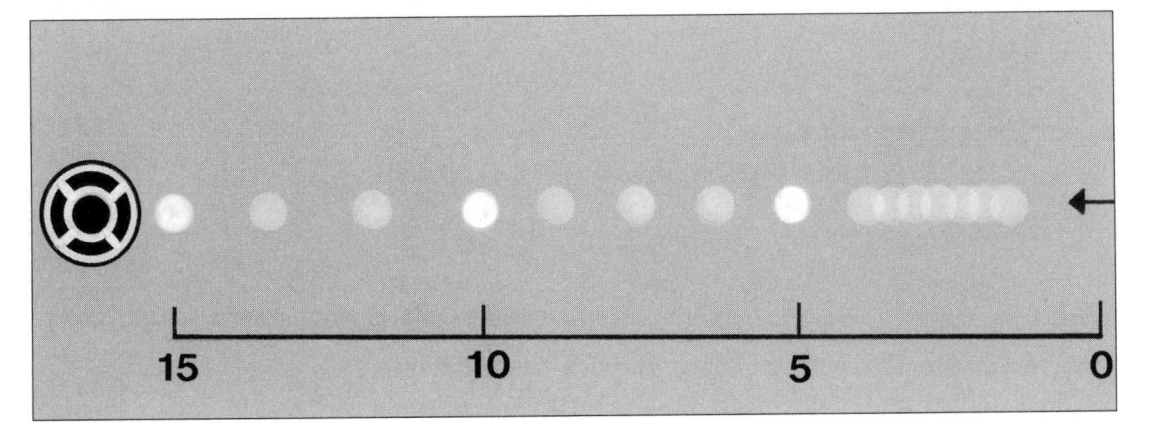

15   10   5   0

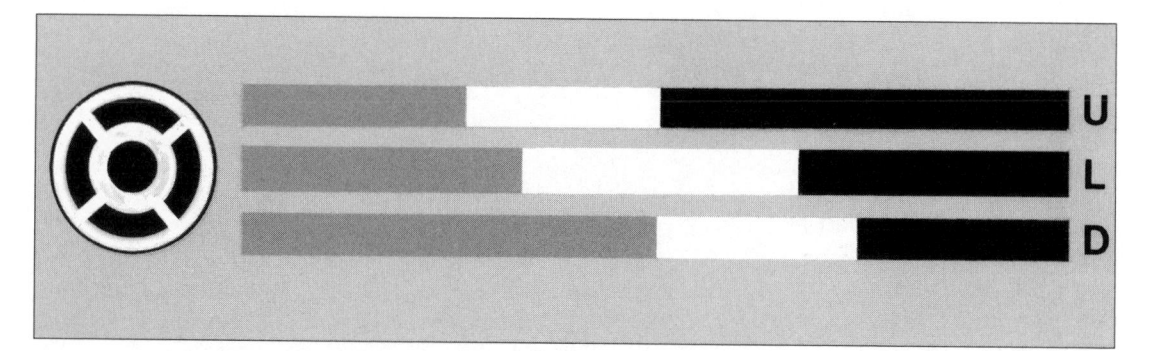

The top strip shows a moderate uphill putt; the middle strip, a level putt; and the lower strip, a moderate downhill putt. The dark area shows the acceleration phase, the white is neutral, and the gray represents the deceleration phase.

passes a fast "scoot" of the ball, as it leaves the putterblade, and stops as the energy of the blow and grain force the ball to settle into a lesser speed. Standing behind the ball, visualizing this phase with your inner eye requires your eyes to rapidly diverge out and away as they imagine the speed of the ball. This registers in the brain and is passed on to the motor system. The pushing of the ball in this phase becomes the energy for the putt.

Clinic attendees found this phase most difficult to imagine. This may be because, when impacting the ball with a lot of energy, as is necessary for longer putts, the golfer finds out that by the time his eyes look up, the ball has traversed several feet.

It is most helpful to watch others' putts to better appreciate the speed of this phase for moderate to long putts. You can make a game of it. Observe someone's putts and attempt to see how quickly you can determine whether the putt is long, short or accurate when it finishes its roll to the target.

NEUTRAL

Somewhere along the path of the putt the ball will start to slow, as acceleration ends and the next phase begins. I call this phase the Neutral phase. (The transition from one phase to another isn't abrupt.) In the Neutral phase the

A side perspective may be the best place to imagine the three phases of speed.

eyes diverge more slowly compared with the first phase. In this phase the eyes feel as though they are gliding (as the ball appears to be) as they continue to diverge farther out toward the target. Here the pushing of the ball is subtle as the momentum of the first phase carries the eyes further out. During this phase, mild to moderate slopes may affect the ball's roll. For downhill putts, the slope can be a factor in all the phases. A giant key here is to let the visual experience these slopes and make necessary adjustments for the final visualization of all the speeds.

DECELERATION

The Deceleration phase occurs when the ball begins to slow when it loses momentum as it nears the hole. Here,

the eyes are slowing in their divergence, as the momentum of the initial phase and the neutral phase gliding is over and the ball is coming to a stop. This phase is vitally important, especially if the terrain changes, such as when there is a drop-off by the hole. Because of the ball speed slowing, the grain and slope often have more affect on the putt's roll.

My players carefully inspect the last four to six feet of the longer putts for any subtleties. This is key to determining the Acceleration phase—how much energy to impart—for the ball to appropriately slow down as it approaches the hole.

The Deceleration phase is appreciated more by positioning one's self behind the cup and seeing the angle and speed with which the ball should be approaching the hole in the last four to six feet. This gives you the shape of the putt and tells you the speed.

The Deceleration phase could start more quickly in a downhill putt than in a level putt of the same distance. There are the unusual times when the ball may be slowing little, if at all, until it hits the hole. We all are familiar with the real steep grades in greens. These cause the ball to keep gaining speed as it continues down the hill. Be sure to take this factor into account. In this situation, a little tap on the ball is all that may be needed to propel the ball to the hole.

These phases may sound confusing. However, I encourage you to start being aware of them as you watch the pros putt on television or your friends on the putting practice green. This skill is too important to ignore.

An Important Point or Two

I can always tell if a player is correctly using visualization (or in-vision-ing) properly by watching his eyes travel

along the imagined path of the putt. If the player takes three seconds to track the intended path for a level forty-foot putt, or if his eyes track along the green in just one speed and arrive at the hole at that speed, he was not visualizing correctly. If, during visualization, the eye muscles are going too fast as they near the hole, the putt has a good chance to end up well past the hole, because the preparatory phase did not match the situation.

The opposite can occur if the eye muscles are slowing too quickly, and they aren't near the hole. If the eye muscles approach the hole with too little speed, the ball may finish well short of the target. In this situation, there was too little energy or speed in the Acceleration phase. Those who constrict space (they are always short on their putts and on the self-tests) often relate that, when they are visualizing, their eyes want to stop short of the target. They report having to force their eyes the extra few feet. This is because the eyes have perceived (projected) the hole as closer than it really is. As a result, the eyes want to travel only as far as their (mis)perception. The extra feet is what the eyes *must* compute and negotiate in order to make the visual processing more accurate. The opposite is true of those who expand space. Their eyes arrive at the target quicker than they expected them to because the target was projected to be farther off than it actually was.

Note:

When the speed your eyes traveled in the initial visualization (or in-vision-ing) appears inappropriate for the situation, you must stop and repeat the visual-motor movement using an appropriate pace.

If you were short with your visualization, don't just say to yourself, "Oh, hit it a little harder for the actual putt."

Using the Inner Eye from behind the cup gives the player another look and can help you with in-vision-ing.

This is not specific enough a direction for the muscles to follow. Always repeat the visualization or in-vision-ing of the proper pace of the putt—or at least attempt to. As you become more experienced, these phases will be more meaningful and appropriate.

Complete the Act

Make sure you finish what you start. In other words, always have your eye muscles end their journey inside the cup. This completes the visual act and gives a positive image to the mind.

Another point of note is to use your practice-green time to your advantage. Avoid the typical mentality of many we have observed, who are interested in making or missing and do not get the maximum from their time. Use your time to adjust to the green's characteristics. If the green is slow, in-vision it as such before you putt the next putt. Make sure to prepare the muscles for action by using your eye muscles to track along the green at the speed the green commands. Don't just hit the ball harder if it is a slow green, for example. To get the most of your practice-green sessions, practice pre-putt preparation instead of banging away, putt after putt, without any visual preparation. Always make your visualization or in-vision-ing match the situation.

Hang In There

The concept of in-vision-ing is possibly the toughest of all my techniques to perfect. But what is often the most difficult to perfect bears the most fruit. In-vision-ing will take practice, because time is one of man's true frailties. The casinos in Las Vegas have no clocks on the wall so as to not remind you of your customary schedule in hopes you will stay to gamble for a longer period of time.

In-vision-ing has the ability to include everyone, even those that believe they have little to no visualization skills. Instead of counting on visualization to imagine a ball rolling toward the target, you can use your visual-motor skills to your advantage in a positive way, no matter how stressful the moment. In-vision-ing is a valuable stimulus

for action. Keep working on this technique for as long as it takes. Whether it is through visualization, or in-vision-ing, always preview the putt in your mind's eye.

Summary

1. Estimate the distance by walking the eyes, then walk the distance.
2. Visualize the roll of the ball that is necessary to get the ball to end its roll near the hole.
3. If visualization fails, in-vision the speed necessary by using your eye muscles to track along the green.
4. To enhance your visualization skills, study the real-time tables.
5. On the practice green and on the course, study others' putts to appreciate the three phases of speeds, when applicable.
6. If your visualization doesn't match the situation, always repeat the visualization to better match the green's characteristics.
7. Always visualize the ball falling into the cup.

8

The Hole Is Seldom the Target

Don't give up. Don't ever give up.

THE LATE SUPREME BASKETBALL COACH, JIMMY VALVANO

YOU ARE READY to putt a forty-footer. You are sure of the actual distance, have visualized the speed and the path, aimed the putter accordingly and are steadied over the ball, confident of the success to follow. Now what could blow this great preparation?

How often is the hole the last target you look at before returning your eyes to the ball to putt? If your answer is that you characteristically look at the hole quite often right before you putt, you are, at least, one down.

Obviously, all ten-foot putts are not the same. A ten-foot uphill putt isn't going to roll the same as a ten-foot downhill or level putt. As you will discover in this chapter, there are several factors, including the slope of the green, that demand the actual distance give way to an *adjusted* distance. Furthermore, on breaking putts, the aim point is almost always outside the hole. If the putter is aimed five inches left of the hole on a left-to-right breaking putt, a last look at the hole may serve to confuse the brain as to which point to stroke toward. Importantly, the last stimulus to the brain is usually the dominant one for the action to follow.

The hole is an inviting target, but almost always, the wrong target to use as a last fixation point.

One of the most challenging aspects on the green, for many of my students, has been to self-direct, or image, a target to putt to other than the hole. Another frustrating challenge revolves around ways and means to negotiate the slopes that occur along the path of the putt. Yet it has been estimated that 75 percent of the putts incurred in a round of golf are not level. If three-quarters of the putts fit into the slope category, it's no surprise that many golfers three-putt so often. When slope is a factor, we need a way to determine the amount it will affect the ball's roll in order to plug it into the distance formula.

At a putting workshop, at Barton Creek Golf Club, in Austin, Texas, I asked a participant what she does to compensate when faced with an uphill putt as compared to a level putt. She quickly offered: "I just hit it a little bit harder." Unfortunately, this approach is too general and misses the specifics necessary for longer putts. An

approach that uses specifics instead of generalities such as "a little bit harder" is necessary for the majority.

To master the long putt, it's critical to adapt the concept that references all putts as level. For instance, a measured eighteen-foot uphill putt may need to be stroked with the same energy as if it were a level twenty-five-foot putt. But, if the hole is the last point of fixation, there is a potential conflict between the eyes, the brain and the body's motor system. If the stroke length is adjusted for a twenty-five-foot level putt, but the eyes are looking at the hole eighteen feet away, this could leave you with a seven-foot second putt. That's because the stroke you employed matched the "actual" versus the "adjusted" distance.

In other words, 75 percent of the time, the inner eye needs to imagine a different target: one other than the actual hole that provides much better direction for the muscles that control the stroke. Unfortunately, because of habit and the fact that the hole is there, this visual guidance technique isn't always so easy to apply.

Measuring the Slopes

A big unknown, and possibly the most difficult distance element for most golfers is the Y-axis factor, or the degree of slope. Evaluating the degree of slope, and where in the ball's roll it affects the putt, is a must. As discussed in Chapter Two, the slopes are categorized as mild, moderate or severe. There are a few occasions when the slope can be extreme, with an elevation difference of four to six feet from the ball to the hole. To start, find the best position to evaluate the slope from the side of the green. From there, attempt to determine, to the best of your ability, the degree of slope.

A *mild* Y-axis slope refers to an elevation difference of

less than a foot from the ball to the hole. This could add or subtract a few feet, possibly 1 percent to 10 percent, to the actual distance, depending upon whether it was an uphill or downhill putt.

A *moderate* slope refers to an elevation difference of one to two feet. This could add or subtract 10 to 30 percent to the actual distance.

A *severe* slope yields an elevation difference from the ball to the hole of over two feet. This could add or subtract 30 to 50 percent, or more, to the actual distance.

Adjustments to the actual distance are also predicated upon where the slope occurs along the ball's path. If the slope occurs more toward the hole, it will have more effect on the ball's roll, because the ball will have started to lose its momentum as it approaches the hole. The X-axis break can also be affected more with this situation.

On level and uphill putts, a slope positioned closer to the ball than the hole will have less effect on the adjusted distance, because the ball will be moving faster as it hits the slope. Think of riding a bicycle up a slope. If you are moving at a fast pace when you hit the hill, you will need less energy to negotiate the hill than if you started to peddle from a standing position at the start of the slope. A

Where the slope is encountered, especially on uphill putts, can make a significant difference in factoring the "adjusted" distance.

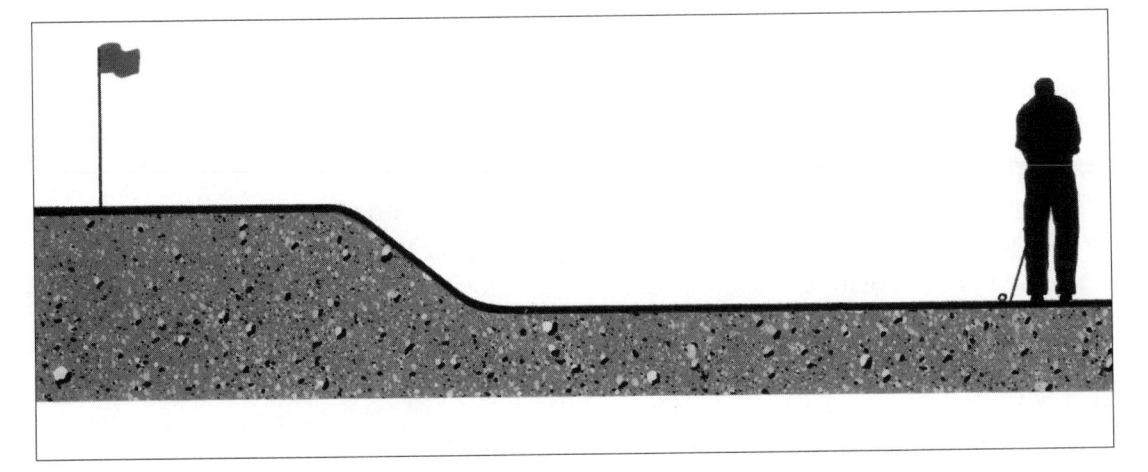

slope in the middle of the ball's path will have a moderate effect on the ball's roll, especially if the putt is downhill-sidehill.

A major component in the Farnsworth System is the appreciation that there are too many factors to make the act of putting as simple as stroking the ball to the actual hole. The hole serves as a reference point for your final target and is there to catch the last shot. But the hole often becomes a distraction from the "real" target—which we refer to as Target B. (Target A is the ball.) Let's look at possible locations of Target B, and why it is used rather than the hole.

Five reasons why the hole is seldom the target are:

1. The Y-axis
2. The X-axis
3. The U-factor
4. Daily adjustments
5. The Pelz Factor

THE Y-AXIS

The Downhill Factor

During a recent Colorado State Senior Four-Ball championship, my playing partner was John Huddy, a low handicapper. We were playing Arrowhead, characterized by undulating and steeply sloped greens. John was having great difficulty on the downhill putts.

Typically, on a twenty-foot downhill putt with a moderate or severe slope, he would roll his ball five or ten feet past the hole. When I looked at his eyes, I saw that his last pre-stroke fixation point was the hole. This made his last stimulus a target that was not appropriate for the slope and grain he faced. By looking at the hole, John allowed his eyes to use the distance from the hole as the last stim-

When faced with a downhiller, do not use the hole as a last fixation point.

ulus for the putt, which served to confuse the brain and tended to negate or ignore the slope's influence on the ball's roll.

A downhill slope serves to sling the ball farther down the hill, thus *decreasing* the effective ("adjusted") distance of the putt compared with a level putt. For a downhiller, gravity reduces the power or energy of the stroke, so a twenty-footer could be more like a fifteen-foot level putt. (Once again, an important key to the degree of adjustment is that one must always use a level putt as a reference.) The last point the player should look at (Target B) becomes a point five feet in front of the hole.

Some severe slopes at Arrowhead would reduce the actual distance by one-half, or even more. This means you

must create an illusion of Target B that will be located much closer to you than the hole's actual location. At times, Target B can be a foot from the ball on a ten-foot putt. This means you hit the ball with only enough energy to get it to a point one foot away from where it sits at address, as if it were a one-foot level putt. Of course, this would be a severe slope and you would need to just get the ball rolling.

Say you walk off the putt (as you should always do for putts over ten feet) and determine that it's a thirty-footer, down a mild slope with little grain. You decide to adjust the distance by 10 percent (1 to 10 percent for a mild slope). This means to reference the putt as a (adjusted)

A moderate or severe downhill putt projects Target B much closer than the actual hole.

level twenty-seven-footer; your last look would be at a point three feet in front of the hole. If the slope were more toward the hole (than a gradual slope), you may wish to adjust the distance by another two or three feet, making Target B a point six feet in front of the hole.

But a moderate-sloped forty-footer may need to be adjusted by 15 percent, making the adjusted distance thirty-four feet (.15 X 40). If the slope is near the hole, a 30 percent adjustment may mean a level putt of twenty-eight feet (.30 X 40 = 12; 40 – 12 = 28 feet). Please realize, this approach is a best "guesstimate," but it's better than shutting off the mind (vision) by always using the hole as the only target. Once more—it is important that one gets used to referencing all putts as level in order to combat the tricks of the green.

A severe sloped downhill thirty-footer could mean subtracting fifteen feet (.50 X 30 = 15) from the actual distance. This could leave an adjusted length of fifteen feet for the location of Target B. You now reference Target B as a level fifteen-footer.

The Uphill Factor

Uphill putts expand space, as gravity creates a drag on the ball. An uphill putt requires more energy, plus a longer backswing and follow-through than a level or a downhill putt of the same length. This is because an uphill putt can add several feet to the measured Z-axis distance. A twenty-footer may need to be adjusted to a level twenty-five-foot putt.

An uphill fifteen-foot putt with little grain and a mild slope may require only a little more distance to be added than a level putt would. So you may decide to project Target B two feet beyond the actual hole. A fifteen-foot uphill putt with a moderate slope may require you, with long grain growing against you, to project Target B as an adjusted, level twenty-footer.

A fifteen-foot uphill putt may need to be played as a level twenty-footer.

A severe slope and heavy grain going against you may require Target B to be projected six or more feet beyond the actual hole. Once again, first attempt to determine the degree of slope, then add it to the measured distance to see how much space has been expanded. Use that amount as the location of Target B. Make a decision. Project Target B past the hole by a certain amount.

A common occurrence at Bear Creek Golf Course in Morrison, Colorado, would be a slightly uphill twenty-foot putt with a moderate, abrupt slope of two feet, with the slope just before the hole. Even though it is a moderate slope, because the slope occurs near where the ball usually starts to slow, it will have more effect on the roll. So you decide to categorize the slope as severe. This means you place the distance in the category to add at

Uphill putts require you to look beyond the hole.

least 30 to 40 percent to the twenty feet. You now decide that the adjusted distance becomes a twenty-six-foot level putt.

Ignoring the hole can be a difficult habit to break. But using the hole as the last stimulus can destroy any proper preparation before this point. At the very least, looking at the hole can confuse the muscles of action. Because the location of Target B is near the hole is difficult to define when behind the ball, it's important to note how far it is away from the hole before going back to behind the ball.

ONCE MORE FOR THE RECORD

Just realizing that Target B is in *front* of the hole on a downhill putt and *behind* the hole on an uphill putt can help you.

Looking at the hole instead of Target B can be misleading to the brain. As my partner John discovered, the hole can be an inviting target. Either he lacked the ability to visualize Target B, or he possibly was using his home course as a reference. In any case, he lost the battle that day. To master the challenge of distance, the hole must give way to an illusion of reality: Target B. Even though my approach is not an exact science, it is better to use a best guesstimate than to ignore these factors altogether.

THE X-AXIS

Steve Elkington barely missed the cut at the 1996 "International" in Castle Rock, Colorado. On Saturday as I was getting ready to do some eye-control drills and practice-green work with Nick Faldo before his round, Steve cornered me and set a time that day for me to test him.

Steve tested well on my visual perception drills, so there were only a few areas that were in need of my assistance. He is a very visually dominant learner in how he prepares for each tourney, and how he prepares for each shot.

We spent about two hours on the practice green, going over routines and my concepts. Steve had already used the logo alignment as a visual guide and found it a great help, especially for the shorter putts. On breaking putts, he was not sure whether his last look was at the hole or at his aim point before he putted, but he admittedly liked the Target B concept. He agreed that it was difficult to ignore the hole. He also was intrigued by the concept that the last point of look could dominate the brain and that this may

throw his putting stroke off the aim point. Steve is close to becoming a good—to great—putter.

A putt that is stroked along a slope, making it somewhat of a sidehill putt, will result in a left or right break from the ball to the hole. This will cause an adjustment in alignment that may, for a mild slope, result in aiming the putterface left or right of the hole by a few inches to a foot.

A moderate sidehill slope may result in the necessity to aim the putter more than a foot outside the hole.

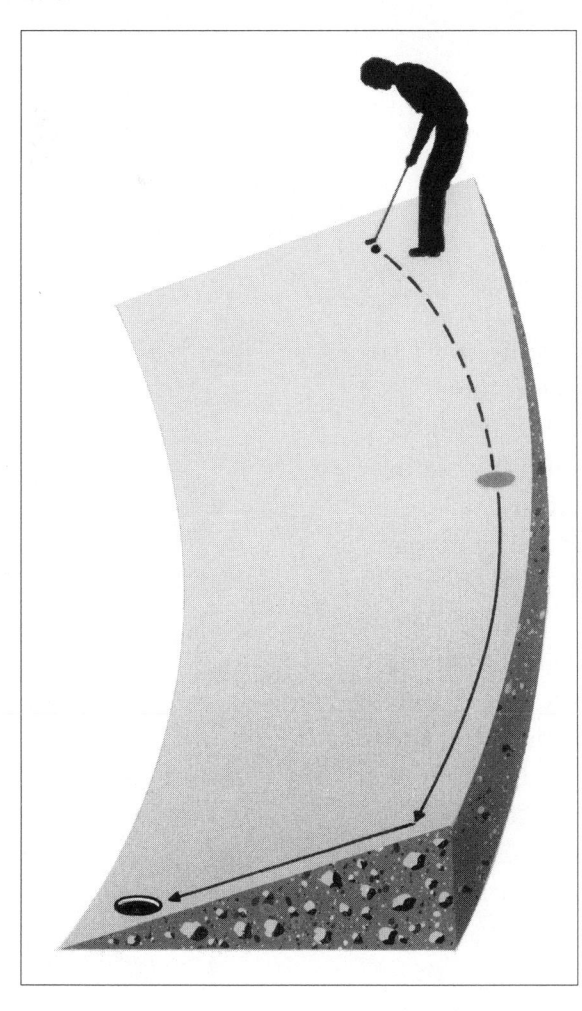

Here, a player projects Target B five feet left and eight feet short of the actual hole.

Arrowhead has several severe slopes that could cause a player to aim their putter five to ten feet left or right of the hole.

A putt that has the higher part of the slope on the player's left, as he looks from behind the ball, will cause a left-to-right break, forcing him to project Target B left of the hole. A slope that has its high point to the right of the player, as he stands behind the ball, causes a right-to-left break. So the player must project Target B to the right of the hole. In essence, barring grain or a double break, a majority of the time the player is aiming into the slope. The key here is to make the last point of looking be the aim point and not the hole. If the hole is the last look, the putterface or the stroke is adjusted subconsciously toward the hole instead of the aim point.

A player may have to project Target B five feet left and eight feet short of the actual hole when faced

with a downhill and sidehill putt. An uphill, sidehill putt
may force the player to project Target B two feet right or
left and several feet beyond the hole.

GRAIN

The putt can also be affected by the grain and the type of grass. Public courses generally have longer nap, to deal with busy traffic. This causes a slowness of the ball's roll, affecting the break less and the speed more. An uphill putt must be adjusted more with long grain running with the slope compared with little grain. If the grain goes against the slope, the ball will break less than the degree of slope indicates. A heavy grain going down the slope can cause a downhill putt to max out the 40 to 50 percent measured adjustment of a severe slope, for example.

A fast green, ironically, causes the ball to travel slower along its route, giving the grain more chance to influence the ball's direction. A slick surface, therefore, *adds* to the degree of the X-axis break. Check in with your personal pro for more specifics in this area. Learn from his knowledge and eye.

THE U-FACTOR

When Nick Faldo and Bernhard Langer were tested, both were amazed that the reason they were coming up short on their putts was not from mechanics, or being tentative, but from their eyes misperceiving the hole's location. If your eyes are not very adept at computing distances into a stroke that fits, or you are especially not able to get the ball to end up close to the hole very much of the time, it is often because of a spatial misperception.

No matter what physical and mechanical skills you bring to the game of golf, you still must include certain personal aspects before any stroke is undertaken. If you

had a "spatial" or "directional" error on the coin toss or especially on your Putting Self-Assessment in the appendix, then you should factor in your typical error. To start, you must always know the actual distance (Z-axis) of the putt. Walking it off is a must in factoring the specifics necessary. Then you must plug in any personal (U-factor) misperceptions.

Z-axis Error

Example 1

Say you were six inches short (your U-factor) at ten feet on the coin toss test. You are faced with a level putt of twenty feet. Your (mis)perception of the hole would project it at nineteen feet. This was derived by doubling your error (six inches), as the putt is twenty feet, or two times greater than the test distance.

$$o \text{———}20'\text{———} O \text{—}12"\text{—} X$$
ball   hole Target B

Example 2

Your U-factor error was twelve inches long at ten feet. A twenty-foot level putt would result in a projection of Target B two feet closer than its actual location.

$$o \text{———}20'\text{———} X \text{—}24"\text{—} O$$
ball   Target B hole

These misprojections may appear to be insignificant. But when you add other factors, the error could result in a comeback putt of several feet instead of several inches. The chart below refers to a twelve-inch and eighteen-inch spatial error for the original ten-foot test distance.

A U-factor error may demand a projected target farther than the actual hole.

A U-factor error may demand a projected target closer than the actual hole.

TWELVE-INCH SPATIAL ERROR	EIGHTEEN-INCH SPATIAL ERROR

A putt of

Twelve-Inch Spatial Error	Eighteen-Inch Spatial Error
10 feet = 12-inch error	10 feet = 18-inch error
15 feet = 18-inch error	15 feet = 27-inch error
20 feet = 2-foot error	20 feet = 3-foot error
30 feet = 3-foot error	30 feet = 4.5-foot error
40 feet = 4-foot error	40 feet = 6-foot error

Keeping this simple, if you are *short* with your tosses, you project the hole closer to you than actual. To compensate, you need to add the amount of error to the distance of the hole. As shown below, a twelve-inch error, translated for a thirty-foot putt, would mean you need to project Target B three feet past the hole (12 X 3).

$$o \text{———}30'\text{———} O \text{—}3'\text{—} X$$

ball   hole   Target B

If you are *long* with your tosses, you need to subtract the amount of error from the actual distance of the hole.

$$o \text{———}27'\text{———} X \text{–}3'\text{–} O$$

ball   Target B   hole

X-axis Error

Alignment errors can be somewhat compensated for by choosing a different target. X-axis (directional) errors are also compounded with the increased distance of the putt. The angle of the putterblade off line increases the amount of error as the distance increases from you to the target. If you were one-quarter of an inch off on the dot test in Chapter One, a ten-foot putt would make your error three inches if you looked at the hole as your aim point.

Three-Inch X-axis Error   Five-Inch X-axis Error

A putt of

10 feet = 3-inch error	10 feet = 5-inch error
15 feet = 4.5-inch error	15 feet = 7.5-inch error
20 feet = 6-inch error	20 feet = 10-inch error
30 feet = 9-inch error	30 feet = 15-inch error

Example 1

On a twenty-foot putt, to compensate for a three-inch X-axis misperception (at ten feet) that is right of the actual target, you need to project Target B six inches to the left. This means you would aim your putter six inches left of the hole on a straight putt.

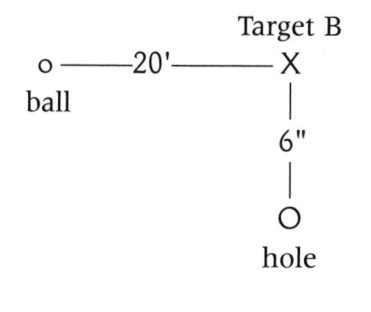

Example 2

If your misperception is left of the actual target, you need to self-direct Target B to the right. Once again, Target B is the last place you should look before referencing the ball.

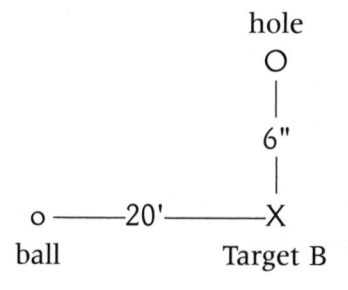

Example 3

Obviously, a five-inch X-axis error demands more significant adjustments. A visual compensation of five feet behind the hole for a spatial error and possibly fifteen inches left is an amount that may be a difficult but necessary projection for Target B.

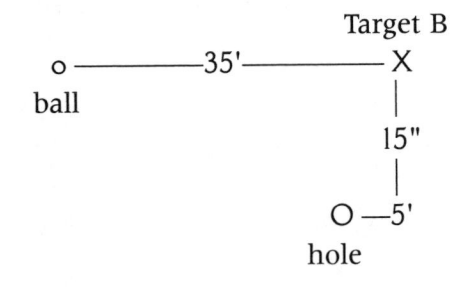

DAILY ADJUSTMENTS

A. If your visual system is inconsistent, the U-factor can vary. I recommend a self-assessment test every day before you play. A convenient test can be used on the putting green. Pace off ten feet from the hole. Face the hole, close your eyes, then toss a golf ball to the hole. Open your eyes before the ball lands to see where you are perceiving the hole today. The U-factor can change for a variety of reasons, including neck and back muscle tightness. As you perfect your skills, there may be a need to recompute your U-factor. This is why pre-round practice on the putting green is so important. Here, you can fine-tune any adjustments before you play. If your putts are short or long of the hole, find a more appropriate Target B to reference.

B. If the greens are fast, move Target B closer than usual. If the greens are slow, move Target B farther back than is customary.

The Pelz Factor

Dave Pelz's research reveals the ball should be going at a speed that would cause it to come to rest seventeen inches behind the hole. This is to help compensate for things such as spike marks, foot prints and the "volcano effect" (from constant foot depressions that cause the hole to rise slightly as the hours or days go by). Even on level putts, you should incorporate the Pelz Factor. This means that you should project Target B at least seventeen inches past the actual location of the hole. Remember, the Pelz Factor always *adds* to the distance component.

It will take time to appreciate the degree of a slope and its effect, but if you attempt to classify each before the putt, you have a better chance to avoid adding another stroke or two to your total. Make sure to make notations in your green-reading diary for future reference. Even if this isn't an exact science, this effort becomes more specific than "hitting it harder." One must plug in the adjusted Z-axis factor to come up with a final distance.

Factoring It All Together

You have a spatial error of one foot short, you have a Z-axis adjustment (for an uphill putt) of three feet, the Pelz factor, and say you have fallen into the trap of the myth of the three-foot circle—you may end up with a second putt of eight to ten feet.

Remember, Target B should be an illusion that compensates for the directional, the spatial and any other factors. Combining the components of spatial and directional U-factor with the other components could end up with Target B eight feet behind and six inches left of the hole on a fifteen-foot putt.

If you project Target B on an uphill putt five feet past

the hole, and that is where you end up, don't blame the system. Give it time. Most often a putt that goes awry is because you are plugging in new factors but still using some old habits, such as hitting it harder (because it is uphill).

You are bound by habits, and they are no more apparent than at a place where you developed them. Certainly, if the course is your home course, plugging in any new formula will take time. It may be wise to take your new knowledge to an unfamiliar course, where a twenty-foot putt needs a closer look.

Summary

The Farnsworth System tasks of mastering distance are as follows:

1. Walk off the distance of the putt, and relook the distance.
2. Analyze the slope and grain in the green's surface.
3. Pick an exact spot for Target B, based on the slope and all other factors.
4. Look at Target B a final time before stroking the ball—the hole is seldom the target!

9

Visual Concentration and Establishing a Game Plan

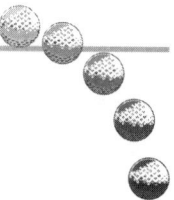

Ninety percent of this game is half mental.

Yogi Berra

Why are some players always in the hunt while others taste only fleeting moments of glory? The answer, in a word, is *concentration*.

Jeff Maggert's four-putt in the 1994 Player's Championship cost him $100,000 in prize money. He missed two consecutive two-footers. Even seeing it on television, it was clear his customary routine broke down.

The primary characteristic among consistent winners on the pro tours is their dedication to a routine. The putting elite stick to the same routine, stroke after stroke, green after green, day after day—regardless of conditions, and whether it's practice or play.

No one single area may be any more important to concentration than the pre-shot routine. So much of the pre-shot routine is visual in nature that we refer to it as visual concentration. It is important to realize that most lapses in concentration are not the result of a breakdown in mechanics, but are derived from the lack of proper

application of the visual sensory system and the lack of quality visual skills. The proper application of concentration and vision is the pre-shot routine, your *game plan* for success.

A routine is the systematic way of applying concentration to the field of endeavor. The timing and order of business can vary, but the key is your consistent use of a set routine. The following is the Farnsworth System: a step-by-step task analysis applied to concentration. Feel free to tailor my game plan to your liking. Be careful to not leave out essential components. My recommendation for a putting routine includes the following:

1. Analyze the controlling factors such as slope and grain.
2. Aim the logo at a target.
3. Walk off the distance.
4. Visualize the path for speed and the line from behind the hole.
5. Locate Target B while you are near the hole.
6. Observe from a "long" perspective.
7. Visualize or in-vision the proper speed from behind the ball, and re-aim the logo if necessary.
8. Take two practice swings that match the energy necessary.
9. Massage the path or Zorro it to pick your spot.
10. Address the ball, first aligning the putter to the spot or logo line.
11. Complete your address position.
12. Take a final look at Target B.
13. Stroke the ball.
14. Replay (your concentration keys).
15. Replay II (if necessary).

Game Plan for Success

A. The Pre-play Phase

My plan for mastering the challenge of the greens through concentration has three phases. The Pre-play phase is the first phase, characterized by the tasks necessary to set the stage for a stroke that matches the situation. Here are the Pre-play tasks.

1. *Analysis starts on the practice green, by noting if the conditions are slower, faster or about the same as what you are used to.* Analyzing on the course begins with the shot positioning to the green and continues as you approach the green. Use your *outer eye* to observe details that relate to alignment and pace of the ball, including the degree of slope and the length and direction of the grain that will determine the distance and direction of Target B. If appropriate, reference your green-reading diary or advice from your playing lesson. Importantly, be of the mind-set to walk on the green as if it were the first time. Look for the slopes and the grain factors. Keep exercising the outer eye skills. Obtain as much information as possible before it is your turn to putt.
2. *Aim the logo according to your analysis of the break (if any).*
3. *Walk off the distance and observe the terrain as you walk from ball to hole.* Especially pay attention to the last four feet or so and whatever appears to be able to influence the putt's direction or speed. Also note the area behind the hole for any drop-off in terrain that may influence the ball's roll if it were to travel past the hole.
4. *Visualize or in-vision the ball's roll from behind the hole.*

This perspective yields a slower, more easily appreciated ball speed as it enters the area of the hole. Utilize pertinent information from task number three combined with your initial analysis. Call upon your inner eye to imagine the ball's roll over the last few feet and see it enter the hole. See the direction it enters the hole and imagine it coming at the hole with the proper speed. This visualization helps predict the aim point of Target B.

5. *Determine Target B near the hole instead of behind the ball.* This is especially crucial for longer putts, as many players have difficulty arriving at an accurate perception from behind the ball. While near the hole, pick a spot to the best of your ability that will approximate the direction the putt must start on and the distance from the hole that the energy must be used. An uphill putt will place Target B past the hole and a downhiller will place Target B in front of the hole. Be specific in terms of an exact spot for Target B's location in relation to the hole, so as to reference it when you move behind the ball.

   Plug in your U-factor (if necessary). If everything is neutral, meaning there are no perception problems and the putt is level, then Target B would be on a straight line from your spot to a point past the hole by seventeen inches (the Pelz Factor). Most importantly, make a decision.

6. *Observe from a "long perspective" for putts over fifteen feet.* Stand below or above the line of the putt, and far enough away to visualize the ball's roll along the entire path. For those who need extra visualization aids, this is a useful perspective.

7. *Visualize or in-vision again from behind the ball.* Because this is such an important component of the preparation process, I encourage my students to again visualize the speed all the way into the hole.

The muscles now have the specific energy necessary to hit the putt to the target.

Standing below and to the side of the ball's intended path can be a helpful perspective.

In the 1994 British Open, Fuzzy Zoeller was contending in the final round. He would analyze the situation and, just before he set up, would walk between the hole and the ball for a last survey of the path the ball was to travel. Once he arrived at the ball, it was no time before he fired away. On that day, Fuzzy couldn't buy a putt from any distance. On the greens he lost his chance for a victory.

Obviously, Fuzzy has had to be a good putter to be a dominant player on the PGA Tour. It is pure conjecture that Fuzzy could improve his putting by

going behind the ball (or the hole) to visualize the speed and direction necessary to get the ball to the hole. But too often using the hole to align to, and especially ignoring the chance to align from behind the ball, is trusting visual perception too much.

Use your inner eye to be specific when visualizing the pre-putt action, including details of tempo, tension level, the specific path and speed of the putt. It is okay to just see the ball's roll in this task. However, if your visualization and analysis tell you there is more break than you initially perceived, re-aim the logo from behind and then re-address the ball. Be sure to attempt to be as accurate as possible on seeing the three phases: acceleration, neutral and deceleration. Seeing is believing.

The new player, while behind the ball, should visually "laser" the path—burn the path—from the ball to the hole. This visual guidance technique impregnates a powerful image from the eyes to the brain to the motor—the "loop."

If visualization fails, use in-vision-ing. If in-vision-ing does not match the situation, make sure to repeat this phase until you perceive it fits the situation. It is important to see the ball go along the path and into the hole. Complete the visual act.

8. *Practice your stroke from beside the ball or behind the ball.* For those with alignment inconsistencies, practicing the stroke from behind the ball (while facing the target) keeps the line of the ball to the distance target fed to the brain. Take two or three practice strokes that approximate the actual stroke you are to make.

Pro Justin Leonard's routine is a model to copy. I particularly like, after his practice strokes, when he goes behind the ball one more time to see his spot or the line. He definitely has a set routine.

It is imperative that the practice strokes duplicate

A practice stroke behind the ball keeps your line or aim-point fed properly to your brain.

the stroke you will be using for the actual stroke. An exaggerated practice stroke that has no relevance to the task could complicate the task. During the practice putts, if there appears to be a mismatch in the energy needed and the speed visualized, by all means step back and take two or more practice swings that match your perception of the energy needed. I encourage my players to look at the hole from behind the ball during their practice strokes, for three reasons: 1) The

eyes are given a distance to relate to; 2) vision is accented while mechanics are ignored; and 3) the eyes are triangulating down the target line.

9. *Align.* Apply the Farnsworth System of alignment that works the best for you, or for the day. You can use the logo or a spot to align to.

Don't look at your far target first.

First align your putter blade to the logo or the spot chosen.

10. *Address the ball.* First align your putterblade to the logo or the spot chosen. Then align your feet and body square to the line. Make sure to align the putter to the spot or the logo, then complete the stance before looking at Target B.

If visual noise is a problem, place the putter down in front of the ball or over the ball before completing the address. Process only the distance target and don't judge the alignment when over the ball. To help with this situation, look from the chosen spot to Target B. Only reference the ball when ready to begin the stroke. If you are still unsure of your alignment, on short putts (seven feet or less), incorporate the "shaft."

Align to the spot by walking on a straight line from behind the ball, then placing the putter down first.

B. THE PLAY OR "SEE-DO"

It must be stressed, the Pre-play phase should be dominated by the visual. If not, the next phase, the Play, is difficult to execute consistently. This is because nothing is more visual than the Play phase of visual concentration. This phase is started when the golfer is over the ball about to start the stroke and finishes when the stroke is finished.

The Play is such an important phase that Chapter 10 is devoted to this moment of truth and ways to obtain peace

of mind and purity of stroke. For now, the Play phase becomes a "See-Do" task. See the (distance) target, see the ball, then do it. It is a time to trust and to execute. It's your time to step to center stage and hit the ball.

11. *Complete your address position.* It is imperative, especially when you are over the ball, that you be time-consistent. The most important time that is exceeded when I observe the less-than-elite is when the player is in the address position. This is because the player is attempting to perform too many tasks. Alignment is done as the player assumes the address position. When the player finishes his set-up, all that is left is to reference the distance target and possibly, for some, the need to see the stroke line. This task should take no more than three to five seconds after the player completes his or her address.

    You need to make a choice in this task. This moment is not about *how* to hit the putt. It is about bringing the two targets—the aim point and distance point—together. And another choice must be made: Stroke it with confidence or choose to be tentative, hoping to die it into the hole because of mistrust of alignment or slope factor.

12. *Take a final look at Target B.* Remember, the goal is to make the putt. But your task, while over the ball, is to *hit the ball from Target A to Target B.* You have programmed your muscles in the Pre-play phase. Once over the ball, it is not a time for second guessing. It is time to fire away with trust.

13. *Stroke the ball.*

C. REPLAY

After all the action is complete, and the ball is on its way, it's time to incorporate a potential key to maximizing per-

formance. Replay asks you to revisit key points of your game plan. By understanding what went right, you have a chance to repeat the good fortune. But unless you know what you did to ensure success, the next effort may be a disaster. This is often the case when a person tends to omit a key point of their game plan.

To maximize the learning process, one must always replay the action by asking four important questions:

A. Did I select the visual (system) during the stroke?
B. Was I in control of my tension level?
C. Did I complete my pre-shot routine?
D. Did I stay positive?

If during the Replay you discover a tendency to omit a part of your game plan, you are potentially leaving learning to chance. If the answers to all four of the above questions were affirmative, then move to the next step. A "no" to any of the above signals means it is time to plug back into the game plan. Let's take a look at these four critical areas of concentration.

It's Visual

If you can honestly say you were visually tuned to the task of hitting the ball while processing only the ball and Target B, you are on your way to mastering visual concentration. Be honest with yourself when assessing these areas. If you were thinking about mechanics or about the outcome, you need to work more on visual dominance.

Tension Level

Replay your tension level in your muscles. Check whether it is proper, not too high or uncontrolled.

After a round of golf, if your hands or arms are tired or

aching, you can bet the tension level was too high. If it is too high, you may be focusing on the goal, or not visualizing properly. Write down in your diary to check your tension level before each shot for the next time out on the course.

Checking Your Routine

Whether the result of the putt was positive or negative, you must score your game plan. In other words, concentration is not a complete success if the putt was made but one or more of the tasks was omitted. Even though the ball went in, you may have opened up an opportunity for failure in the future by skipping a part of your routine. If a task is omitted often, make a note in your diary to focus on this aspect in your pre-round visualization and during actual play.

Staying Positive

The next step of the Replay stage is to ask "What did I perceive just before my performance?" "Was I using Target B as a positive, or can I honestly say my subconscious interfered by picturing a negative of what not to do?" Avoid thoughts such as "Don't three-putt." Visualize the ball going into the hole. See success.

If all the above were correct, then you have exercised concentration to the best of your ability.

Replay II—Your Final Place to Stay Positive

Replay II gives you a last chance to leave the green with a positive attitude. After replaying the four questions, make amends for any loss of concentration. See yourself properly implement the four key areas of the Replay. When

possible, you should see yourself in your mind's eye going through the omitted portion(s).

Replay II also has you picture yourself making the putt. Always take the time to imagine stroking the ball again and *see* it go in the hole. If this is difficult, in-vision the path the ball should have traveled to end up in the hole. Picturing the positive after the fact occupies the mind with a positive, and acts as a confidence-builder for the future. If you repeat this step a couple of times, your mind has more positives to deal with than negatives. The mind does not separate fact from fiction.

It is possible an erroneous assessment of the slope may be the cause of a missed putt. If so, relook the slope factor when you complete the hole. Never leave the green with a negative picture. Always see the positive.

Do the great putters go through all of these tasks? Probably not. But once again, until your perceptions are great, stick to the basics. Routines vary, but the elite have a consistent routine. The Tour players, when it is their turn to putt, try to complete their routine and get the stroke off in under thirty-five seconds.

Now it is time to go out to the course and start to work on a consistent routine. Or is it?

A Practice Ground

If a new technique is brought to the course without it first being somewhat automatic, there is a great chance of the technique becoming a distraction. This especially applies to the pre-shot routine. Pre-round visualization with the inner eye is the most valuable place to initially practice the pre-shot routine.

Imagine playing your last round of golf and revisiting each putt. With stopwatch in hand, plug in all of the steps to the game plan routine, including any assessment of the

green after it is your turn to putt. If the time exceeds thirty-five seconds, look to see what is taking too long to execute. Most often it is the analysis phase. The pros learn to do much of this before it is their turn. When they are on the clock, they usually have only to walk along their intended path, assessing particularly the last few feet of the putt and visualizing the ball's roll as they walk. They spend the rest of their time seeing the line and practicing the stroke necessary.

10

The Moment of Truth

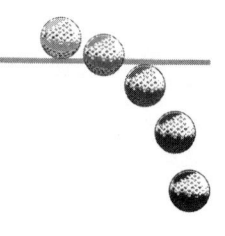

Thinking and analyzing while you are seeing doesn't really help; in fact, thinking hinders the seeing process.

W. TIMOTHY GALLWEY, *THE INNER GAME OF GOLF*

AS THE PLAYER STANDS over the ball, ready to pull the trigger on an eight-footer to win the club championship, it all comes down to a fleeting few seconds that ultimately determine agony or ecstasy. During this time, the mind can be focused on the task at hand or appear to draw upon every negative putting experience from previous rounds.

Some players focus appropriately, while others find their emotions and imaginations run wild. Despite careful pre-stroke preparations, it can all go to heck in a split second during the actual stroke. How can you best concentrate on the task at hand during the moment of truth?

This chapter focuses on ways to help you understand the keys to dealing with pressure and performing well on the greens.

Selective Attention and Self-distraction

In the 1992 "Grand Slam" at the PGA West course, Nick Faldo appeared as if he were bothered by every noise and

movement around him. In fact, bad concentration, more than a bad swing technique, was responsible for his last-place finish.

Through testing and interaction with thousands of athletes over the years, the cause of lost concentration has become clear. Too often when a player suffers an error under pressure, the first resort is to look for a person or thing to blame. The truth of the matter is that the player should look no farther than himself. But what to look for, and why, has long been a reason for discussion among the intellectuals of the game.

The reasons we do things well or poorly often lie with the sensory system we select. *Selective attention* means focusing on the best sensory system for the task. What you select most often is your dominant sensory system. But if it isn't the visual sensory system, trust me, it isn't the most effective system for concentrated play on the golf course. The following discussion may be as profound for the mental side of the game as any ever in print.

Recent research tells us that our brain has a gate that modulates the information that it considers relevant. "Gating" the appropriate information for the task, and the ability to control the information that reaches one's brain, is paramount to avoiding self-distractions that can greatly interfere with green-reading and the putting action itself.

Avoiding self-distraction begins with control of our information-processing network or *sensory* systems: auditory (hearing), tactile (touch), visual, proprioception (angles of joints), balance, gustatory (taste) and olfactory (smell).

Our sensory systems measure some type of energy. Any receptor, when stimulated, is acted upon by an energy change. The eye measures radiant energy; the ear measures vibrations; the olfactory, gas energy; gustatory, chemical energy in the nature of sweet, sour, salty or bitter; balance, gravity; and proprioception, joint flexion. The

tactile measures pressure. The stimulus is transferred to chemical and electrical energy in the body's cells and the synapses. The accuracy and efficiency with which this energy is measured by the systems determines how successfully we come to terms with environmental demands.

These systems measure the environment for informa-

The brain often goes into sensory overload when the "gate" is left wide open.

tion that, in turn, prompts responses from the motor system. They can also be self-activated, as is visualization. But they can serve to distract and disrupt concentration if the wrong one is selected.

The most important point is that you *cannot process in two sensory systems effectively at one time*. In other words, a choice must be made: a selection of the best system for the task. Most often, the visual is the correct system to select. Putting is too visually demanding to be complicated by the use of other systems. Once again, you *can* change your gating to the one system the best putters rely on.

During the Grand Slam, Faldo spent too much time "open-gating" the auditory system. That is why he complained of every little noise. He simply gated the auditory system and ignored the visual. His awareness of movement was caused by a lapse in his fine-tuning ability.

Understand, all the sensory systems have a place and are important. But it is equally important to understand that vision can't be shortchanged or placed on automatic pilot.

A key to understanding selective attention can be demonstrated by a question I ask my students. How long does it take, while driving from your house to the golf course, before you quit paying attention to the road and your surroundings? Most admitted, not long. They even wondered whether certain traffic lights were red or green when they drove through them.

If the typical reason for distractions when driving is the radio, one is *listening* to music instead of *seeing* other vehicles and traffic lights along the way. We use the subconscious to start the car, turn it at a corner, change lanes and do numerous things when no conscious thought is necessary to think about how to perform such functions. But a problem can arise if we overload the subconscious by daydreaming. Creating a better balance between the conscious and the subconscious can keep the mind from wandering from the task, and avoid a self-distraction.

Another example of selecting the wrong system (and self-distraction) occurs in reading. How often do you find your eyes at the bottom of the page whose contents you don't remember at all? Both the driving and reading examples demonstrate how going blind visually can cause decreased concentration. The point here is: Vision is the wrong system to place on automatic pilot.

YOU CAN'T THINK AND ACT AT THE SAME TIME

Under the heading of Selective Attention is an otherwise admired activity that we rightly place the blame on for self-distraction: thinking. Thinking is really a self-stimulation of the brain that results in a mental activity that either relates or does not relate to what you are attempting to accomplish. A thinker uses his cognitive skills to plan his approach to the game. But gating thinking has a downside when one should be observing. Uncontrolled thinking can result in daydreaming. When you are attempting to read or drive, or when you are on the course preparing for your next shot, gating vision, instead of daydreaming, helps you pay attention. By staying in the present time longer, you pick up environmental keys, such as interpreting the slope of the green or noting the direction of the grain in it that you may otherwise miss.

In extreme cases, the mind is actually thinking at pitch peak when action should be dominant. One wonders if this applies to Curtis Strange's collapse on the final three holes during the 1995 Ryder Cup matches. During a post-round interview he said that he knew, after looking at the leader board on the 15th hole, that his match was important and from then on he wasn't the same golfer as he was on the previous holes. Thinking about three-putting or the importance of the putt or winning can also override vision's direction of the target.

*Sensory overload!
One must select the system
that is best for the task at
hand.*

How Feel Can Make You Go Blind

"I just don't have any feel today on the greens." You've heard this, or said it yourself.

The great Bobby Jones once said about putting: "It is wholly a matter of touch, the ability to gauge a slope accurately and, most important of all, concentrating on the problem at hand, that of getting the ball to the hole, and nothing more." This statement references well the task we

face in putting. But I challenge his idea that "gauging a slope and concentrating on the problem at hand" is "wholly a matter of *touch*," or *feel*. Somewhere back in time, the sensations that a golfer felt when over the ball, readying to stroke a putt, were labeled "feel." The concept of feel, because it is often erroneously applied to performance, quite possibly may be the greatest single detractor to concentration and putting consistency.

In deference to Mr. Jones and others, let us set the record straight. Feel should not be the stimulus for the motor response to follow. What the body senses or experiences before the putt is a result of a visual stimulus, not a tactile one. CBS golf announcer Peter Kostis was playing in a season-ending pro-pro tournament in Vail, Colorado, partnering his on- and off-air pal, Gary McCord. Peter shot a respectable 69 the first day in 40-degree weather. The second day, on the second hole, a gust of wind came up and blew his right contact lens out of his eye. Unfortunately, it was out of his dominant eye. "Craig, it didn't bother me so much on the long game, but around and on the greens, it left me with no touch. My first putt afterward was a forty-footer and I left it fifteen feet short!"

Physiologically, by definition, the tactile system provides feel or touch. It gives the player information when he picks up a new putter. The tactile measures the weight of the putter and relates it to what the player is currently using as a comparison. The player feels the difference between the new and the old. The tactile system also gives feedback as to the hand pressure you put on the club. A tight grip can freeze the muscles, and too light a grip can cause the putter to slip out of your hands. The tactile relies on past comparisons to tell if the grip pressure feels the way it should when we are putting our best. The tactile is an important system. But it can be disruptive and inappropriate, because it often represents excessive muscle tension, nonspecific information and a means to destroy visual dominance.

Excessive Muscle Tension

In one of my seminars, a mini-tour professional had a hard time believing she should give up on the feel concept. After all, she "always played by feel." She was asked to make three coin tosses at a target, accenting feel. Next, she was asked to picture the desired path of the coin before the toss, then throw to the target. She was much more consistent the second time.

Feel can be a catalyst for excessive tension for a golfer. Our muscles can only contract or relax. When accenting feel, the tactile's first response is often a muscle overcontraction. A contracted muscle is difficult to control. Moreover, it does not yield the consistency necessary for putting excellence.

The challenge to toss three pennies, emphasizing feel, can cause a muscle tightness in the arm. Elevated or excessive tension in the motor system may cause an abrupt or automated putting stroke, both of which can result in a problem with the speed of the ball. Too much tension can result in a pulled putt if the muscles in your right hand contract and close the blade at impact.

The pro admitted to having an erratic putting stroke. After our discussion, she realized it may have been partly the result of muscle contractions brought on by accenting feel. Tactile selection may be responsible when a ten-foot putt ends up three feet short or a fifteen-foot putt ends up six feet past the hole. Both can be the result of the muscles tightening from selecting feel.

Less Than Specific

Dave Pelz's research proved that the tactile system is much less a specific processing system than previously thought. By covering up the player's eyes so that they could not see the flight of the ball, they were woeful at predicting where

the ball went by feel alone. The coin tossing exercise also demonstrates the generalities of feel compared with visual dominance.

In actuality, the visual system surveys the situation and transfers the information to the brain through a chemical reaction that travels along the optic nerve. The brain activates the muscles that are to be used by loading them with an electrical charge. This loading is an activation of the muscles with a certain amount of power for the task. *The feel you experience as you get ready to putt is an energy flow from the eyes to the muscles.* In other words, all of this starts with a visual stimulus.

The quicker you can get into the *see-do* mode, the quicker your putting stroke is allowed to happen. When the stimulus is visual—vision driving the motor—motion has a better chance of being coordinated, efficient and effortless. For example, your pro has noted a tendency toward an outside-in putting stroke that results in your cutting across the ball at impact. Instead of feeling the proper stroke, I recommend you *see* the proper stroke with your inner eye. By seeing where the club is to go, at least you stay visually dominant. The same applies if you are attempting to take the club back less and follow through more to eliminate deceleration of the stroke through the ball. *See* the length of the backswing and follow through.

The late Dr. Elliott B. Forest, famed optometric lecturer and author, stated well the impact of changing your dominant system when he said, "Change an individual's mode of representation and you literally alter his perception of the world. Change his view of what *is* and you automatically change his ability to experience, analyze and respond to his world. By being an effective information-processor of vision, an individual has a better chance of becoming a better achiever: more alert, more attentive, more aware and more alive."

Now, let's look at the next step to gaining control over the situation by controlling one's concentration.

Preparing for the Moment of Truth

Understanding selective attention has had a major impact on the concentration aptitude of many of the athletes I have had the pleasure of working with. Through the selective attention concept and the dissection of the skills necessary to excel in putting, the selection of the visual sensory system is paramount in controlling self-distraction. Vision is also a major key during the action of the putting stroke as well as preparing for the moment of truth. Unfortunately, this does not provide the answer for all.

Many players are unable to shut out the demons of the subconscious. They let the goal of making the putt, or the fear of missing, override the present-time task. The result: The purity of the stroke and the ability to stay with the task—that of hitting the ball from Target A to Target B—is interfered with. To be a consistent winner and handle the pressure of competition, the golfer must find a way to be under control during the moment of truth.

Energy System Running Out of Control

Under the pressure of competition, or when the outcome is on the line, some players find their mind is whirling so fast that they cannot control random or negative thoughts during the stroke. For some, the palms get so sweaty that they have to wipe their hands on a towel or their pants in order to grip the club properly. Others can feel and hear their heart pounding hard enough it seems as if it were trying to escape from the chest cavity. Still others act as if their very existence were threatened and they almost start to shake as they approach the moment of truth. This inability to relax the mind and body is often no more than the energy system running out of control. The player reverts from the out-of-body experience of

paying attention to the environment for cues, of seeing what is to be done using the inner eye, and goes into the body. This creates a sense of doubt and anxiety that runs the emotional gauntlet, and a loss of the tension control that allows the body to lose its motor control. With this comes little to no chance to deal with the moment of truth.

I will now discuss six ways and means to deal with the mental and physical challenges that must be under control, even before the player steps into the address position.

1. Talking One's Way Through the Routine

We have discussed the importance of the pre-shot routine or game plan. A favorite sports psychology technique for present-time control is for the player to talk his way through the routine. This keeps the player focused on each task by accenting it verbally through inner speech. The self-talk "conversation" would go something like this: "It's putting time. I love this part of the game. This is where it is at and I am ready to make it happen. Okay, it's analysis time, big boy. Let's take a look from the best view. Looks like this is the top area. . . Now lets take a look at the last few feet of this putt. What do we have here? No surprises but the drop off behind the hole makes me want to not charge this putt. Let's see this putt's roll. Okay, time to step up. Putter down at my target. Feet aligned, target in sight, grip comfortable, head over the ball, a look at Target B's location. Okay, I can see it in my mind's eye. Let's see my path. Let it go."

This constant chatter to one's self must be positive. My only problem with this approach is its keeping the person from being visual. Yes, you can switch back and forth from thinking and the auditory to the visual, but it can be a tough assignment.

2. Taking In the Pure and Letting Out the Poisons

Taking a deep breath and letting out the air is used universally in all sports, either before or during the action. The world-class shooters use it for concentration by emptying all their lungs' capacity just before they fix their sights on the target. A deep breath helps the player take in fresh oxygen for the system and let out the used. The system is, in a way, purified for action. This type of breath control can be both a part of the preparation and the moment of truth over the ball. The player can exhale, then start the stroke, or start the stroke as they exhale in a slow, controlled fashion. Many believe the relaxation, brought on by a deep breath, is vital to begin a visualization under pressure.

3. Seeing the Positive

There is nothing more relaxing than a vivid visualization of the ball's roll into the hole before the putt is instituted. Positive visualization is paramount for good concentration. Some use this technique twice: once as the finish of the complete visualization of the putt, and again, just before stroking the ball by seeing the last few feet of the projected roll, with the ball *always* dropping in the cup.

4. Present-Time Count

The *Autogenics* routine, developed in Bulgaria several years ago, is an excellent way to calm the mind. It involves a four-count process of counting one's breathing in a one second per count. The inhale phase has the person taking in equal amounts of air for each of the four counts, with the last breath filling the lungs fully. The hold phase has the person holding their breath for the four counts (four seconds). The exhale phase has the person expelling their breath equally for all four counts so that the last exhale

voids the lungs. The hold of four counts is repeated. The cycle is repeated as many times as the person desires. If the person was counting out loud (this isn't necessary and can be counted silently), it would sound like this: "Inhale, two, three, four; Hold, two, three, four; Exhale, two, three, four; Hold, two, three, four."

This technique of controlled breathing can almost instantaneously lower the heart rate and depress subconscious control. It appears least effective when the player has let his energy level get too out of control. Use it just before you get to the green and anytime thereafter. Players tell me they have used it three, four or five times on the same green when they feel the pressure mounting.

A preferred time to use the autogenics or deep breath techniques is just before the act of visualization. If calming the mind is a problem while over the ball, we would like to see the player use the techniques just before walking up to a crucial putt. But these techniques can be utilized anytime a player experiences his energy level above what is desired. For example: Autogenics can be instituted as the player is waiting his turn to putt, and a deep breath can precede the visualization step of the game plan.

5. Tension Control

Keeping a proper energy level is paramount to use the muscles effectively. Before the player gets into the address position, the player is to tighten the grip on the putter's handle as firmly as possible. Hold this tension for a couple of seconds, then lighten the grip on the handle to the grip pressure that you desire. This helps decrease the tension directly in the muscles of action. This technique can be incorporated with deep breathing. As the lungs are filling with air, the grip can be tightened. When the lungs expel the air, the grip can be loosened simultaneously. This combined technique can also be utilized when the player is at address.

6. The Laser Eye Shift

This is a most favored technique of mine, given to me by my mentors, and has seen college students decrease or eliminate "test anxieties" and players handle situations that previously had their minds spinning out of control.

To appreciate this technique fully, try to remember a particularly anxious moment. If possible, sit back for a moment and recreate that level of anxiety. Next, choose an object to the left of your field of vision, such as the corner of the wall. In your right visual field choose another fixation target. Make sure the two targets are several feet apart. The technique: While keeping your head still, shift your eyes back and forth from one target to the other, as fast as you possibly can, for five to ten seconds.

You may notice, it is very difficult to think of anything else or to become preoccupied with other thoughts. This is because the visual sensory system locks you into the present, keeping you from processing thoughts relating to the past or the future.

This simple, but profound technique is valuable, whether you're preparing to tee off or sink a crucial putt. Use the tee markers or two spots on the green, such as the ball and the hole, as fixation points. You can do this just before approaching the ball, while over the ball or whenever you want to rid yourself of any negative thoughts.

The Laser Eye Shift helps keep the other sensory systems at bay when you are in the visual sensory system. Physiologically, during a saccadic—a rapid eye shift—it's difficult to process anything else. This mind-clearing technique was developed by Drs. Lee and Harrison, in the early 1970s, in their work with the Kansas City Royals. Their decision to emphasize visual dominance as the linchpin of performance made Lee and Harrison true pioneers in their field.

Self-control During the Moment of Truth

Now for the stroke itself. These one to two seconds of action deliver the ball to the intended target—either with confidence or with a degree of anxiety.

Several techniques can be valuable in calming the mind during the stroke. One or more may work the best for you. These techniques offer the golfer a chance to control the mind and, in turn, enhance the ability to render a smooth, controlled, accurate stroke during the pressure of concentration.

As discussed, accenting mechanics at the wrong time leads to a disruption of the tension control and muscle fluidity. Standing over the ball and gating the tactile or proprioceptive systems to accent the mechanics of the stroke can also result in the loss of visual direction to see the location of the target. The location of the target not only can more precisely guide the motor system to deliver the correct energy to the stroke, but it can also be vital to concentration, especially during the moment of truth.

Automatic Pilot—Friend or Foe?

We have all faced times when we hear the little whispers of the mind when putting. It is amazing the degree to which unrelated subconscious thoughts can disrupt concentration as we prepare to putt. Ben Hogan admitted to becoming frozen over the ball when putting in his later years. Many a player has confessed to being unable to pull the trigger.

A concept that may well contribute to this loss of self-control is that of "automatic pilot." Golf traditionalists have encouraged the players to think of nothing. To achieve automatic pilot, we depend upon repetition. Repetition builds confidence, but it can decrease concen-

tration and awareness, especially if visualization is denied. Granted, during the swing, mechanics should eventually be set in the subconscious to be trusted. But we can be betrayed by the concept that automatic pilot is the zenith of peak performance. We think of our subconscious as having a vast capacity, and it does. But it is not able to just pump relevant commands regarding physical movement rapid-fire into our conscious brain. That isn't its nature.

You are faced with making a six-foot level putt on the 18th hole to win your flight in the club championship. Can you trust your subconscious to impart a good stroke, without thought or anxiety, by thinking of nothing or avoiding thoughts of the mechanics of the stroke?

Unfortunately, being too much on automatic can cause the subconscious mind to overload. Becoming brain-locked leads to random or negative thoughts. Among other reasons, automatic pilot can lead to a visual loss of the location of the target on the green, leaving the muscles to perform a less-than-accurate stroke!

The Target B Technique

It can become difficult to hold the energy in the muscles after visualizing or in-vision-ing the putt. To gain better control of the energy necessary to stroke the ball to the target and, more important, control subconscious random thoughts, one should always project the location of the target into their mind's eye. This technique requires you to visualize a distance target on the green, in your mind's eye, while fixating on the ball during, or right before, the stroke. Again the visualized target is Target B, while Target A is the ball. As discussed in Chapter Eight, Target B's location changes, depending upon several factors. While simple sounding, the Target B technique can overcome self-distractions and control the mind.

Once you have determined the location of Target B, that point becomes the last point the eyes fixate upon before they look back at the ball. By looking back at this point, the eyes give the brain and the motor system direction and energy to get the ball to the spot. By seeing Target B in your mind's eye, the conscious mind is in control and the subconscious is not allowed to dominate. Implementing this technique in the right sequence can serve to overcome immobilization over the ball (often because the player is standing over the ball too long, allowing time for negatives to surface). Just before the stroke, look at Target B, then back to the ball. When you see Target B in your mind's eye,

Seeing Target B with the inner eye helps control the subconscious demons.

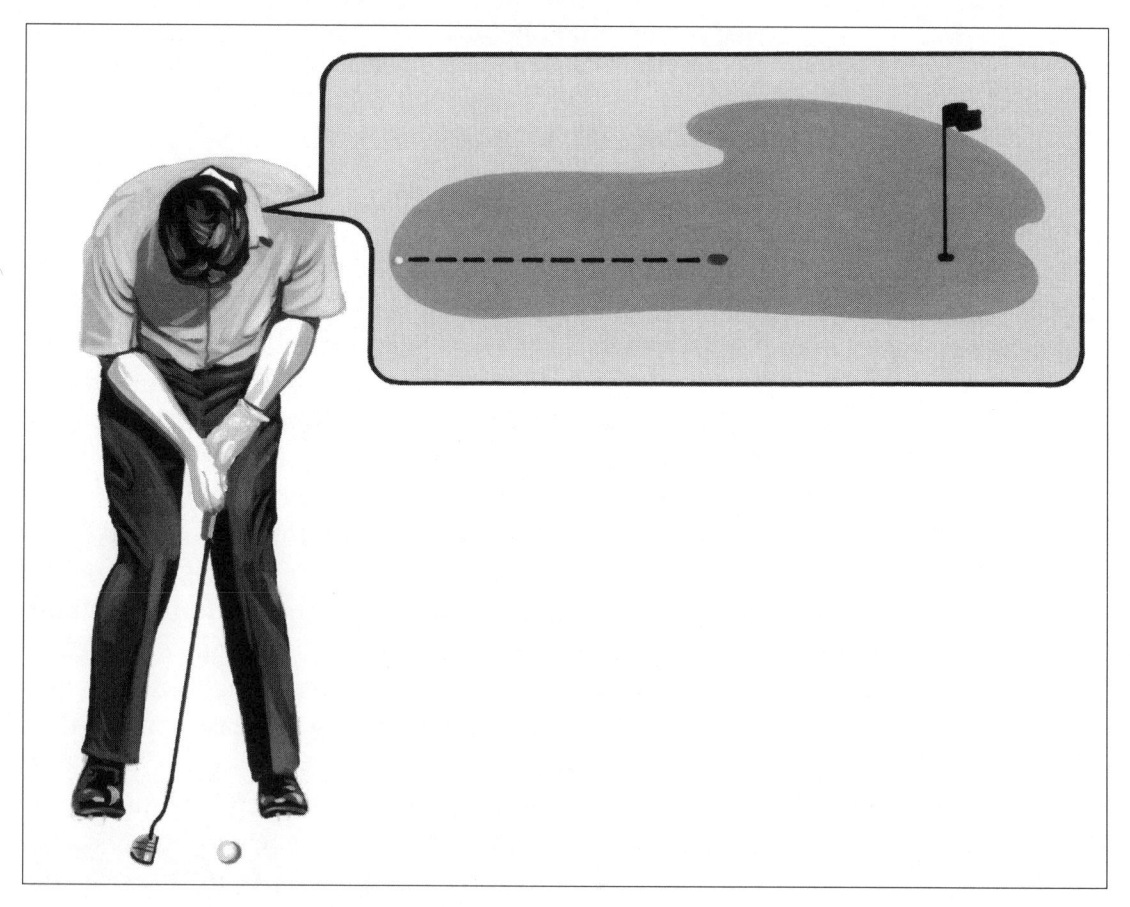

fire away. Remember to keep the target in your mind's eye throughout the stroke. As you perfect the accuracy of the location of Target B, you will find it acts like a homing device, like a radar that helps you lock onto the target. This inner eye technique is a visual guide for the motor to follow. The Target B technique can come to the rescue by overriding the subconscious mind's thoughts of what may go wrong (like three-putting). Rather, you give your conscious mind a positive visual target to pay attention to. Target B should be the last stimulus you receive before looking at the ball. Keep seeing your target even as you stroke the putt. By seeing Target B in your mind's eye, you also decrease emphasis on the mechanics of the stroke. That's important, because mechanical thoughts can also interfere with visual dominance.

Comfort Zone

A favorite technique to rid the mind of the pressure of the moment has to do with using the inner eye. By imagining a comfortable place where one is slowly drifting about in a boat on a quiet lake with the sun beating down, a feeling of warmth and content can override the pressures of the day. Using the same imagination "trick" when readying to stroke that all important putt can take you out of that all-too familiar fear-of-failure mode and calm the mind.

Practice putting to no target on the putting green has a sort of "comfort zone" to it. We stroke the ball without worrying about missing it. Spend five minutes each time putting to "nowhere." This situation usually results in a smooth, confident stroke, namely because there is no penalty for missing.

It is most helpful to recreate the peaceful solitude of the putting green, in the mind's eye, whenever you are standing over a most crucial putt that starts to wear on the

emotions. This is best implemented after you have located Target B and look out at the target. You can, in your mind, place yourself on the putting green. By imagining this is just another putt on the practice green, you actively place the conscious mind in control. The key becomes using the actual location of Target B as the stimulus while placing the mind on the practice green. This combines the reality of the putt with the imagination of the comfort zone.

Believe it or not, you do not have to be an excellent visualizer to apply this technique. Its effectiveness has to do more with your being somewhat calm before the address position is assumed, and this can be aided by the techniques already described for pre-shot preparation. Practice this visual approach whenever possible.

Fine-tune

Chapter Three discussed that using a smaller target to fine-tune the eyes could deliver a more exacting blow and reduce mis-hits. Fine-tuning on a spot on the ball can also exact more benefits.

I have demonstrated time and again in workshops the ability of the eyes to shut down the subconscious through the technique of fine-tuning. I ask participants to think of an anxious moment. When they can feel the anxiety or the mind running out of control, I ask them to look at a small spot, such as a point on the carpet or underneath my eye. They are amazed, even though this is only for a second or two, that they are not processing anything else at that moment but looking at the spot. They are immersed visually and, once again, the mind is controlled.

This second or two of mind control can be extremely useful during the stroke. If you attempt the preceding two recommendations and find them difficult to implement, you may find looking at the back apex or a dimple on the

back of the ball an excellent way to shut out self-distractions. Because you cannot focus intently for too long or too hard, the best time to implement this technique is just a split-second before the stroke begins. Look at Target B to get the stimulus for the muscles, then look back at the ball. As you look back, pick a dimple on the back apex of the ball. The moment the dimple is located, it's time to begin the stroke.

I Need My Mechanics!

By seeing the stroke in their mind's eye during practice putts and the actual stroke to hit the ball, players are given a way to control the mind using a visual stimulus to direct the stroke. Additionally, the player can squeeze and loosen his grip at address, as discussed in the preparation phase, preferably as he is locating Target B. Also, just before the stroke, he can take a deep breath, exhale and then execute the stroke with empty lungs. Nick Faldo whistles a familiar tune as he approaches the ball and while over the ball. He also keeps his mouth open to relax his face and, in turn, relax his body.

Summary

In summary, preparation for the moment of truth includes:

1. Avoiding self-distractions by staying visually dominant.
2. Utilizing techniques such as:

   • Talking your way through your routine.
   • Taking a deep breath.
   • Seeing a positive.

- Doing the four-count breathing drill.
- Arriving at the proper tension control through your grip.
- Using the Laser Shift.

During the moment of truth, you can:

1. Place mechanics on automatic pilot (vision actively sees Target B).
2. Project practice-green image and comfort with your inner eye.
3. Fine-tune your vision as the stroke begins.
4. See your stroke.
5. Use breath control.
6. Trigger the stroke when the eyes arrive back at the ball.

Putting Potpourri

Practice Green Mentality

Tom Kite was on the putting green, practicing before his match with Ben Crenshaw that was being filmed for the *1996 Shell Wonderful World of Golf* series. The venue was the Cypress Creek Golf Course, at Champions, in Houston, Texas.

I watched Tom hit three balls to each hole. He simply stepped up to each one, then fired away. Often the first, and many times the second, missed their target. The third fell in on the ten footers often enough, but this was because of what I call *motor practice*.

Tom called me a week after the match. "Well, Craig, you got to see Ben play some marvelous golf." "Tom," I replied, "You outhit him from tee to green on almost every hole. I think your putting let you down, starting with your approach on the practice green."

I realized I hadn't made it clear previously that he should work on aiming each and every practice putt. We discussed the need to make practice more effective. I told him: "Every putt should be acted upon as if it were on the course, especially in regards to aiming the logo line, but also in regards to green reading and several other components. If you read the putt incorrectly, relook the putt. Work to read the green correctly. Check your notes to see

whether the high point of the course, east-to-west grain, slope-to-grain ratios and other factors are true to form. If not, pay attention to factors that are affecting the putts. Fine-tune your eyes."

I recommended Tom start with the three-coin putting drill, and if putts are missed, then it is time to spend a few moments on the putting stroke before addressing another ball. This gives the eyes, as well as the brain and the motor, a fine-tuning.

The practice green becomes the final lesson for "the loop" before appearing on the *stage*. How you manage your time can be key to accomplishing the most possible or sometimes the least possible. I believe one must eliminate the mentality that your time should be based on making putts versus missing putts. Practice time could be better served by setting goals that would allow one to focus on different aspects of putting, rather than attempting to perfect the imperfect.

I like for my players to start and end their putting session with short putts before they hit the course. Not only does this start and end their time with a fine-tuning of their aiming skills, but it also yields confidence that allows for a comfortable stroke out on the course. Additionally, it can be a time to practice shutting down thinking and adopt a see-do mentality.

Players must also use their practice time to check their accuracy of the Target B projection. Are they short or long on their moderate to long putts because of personal perceptions and/or the green's characteristics? If so, adjust Target B's position and work to master this position for confidence and carryover to the course. This means that a portion of the pre-game putting practice time must also encompass enough time to practice moderate to long putts as well as breaking putts. Most tour players give themselves twenty minutes, minimum, on the putting green. For most players, I would like to see thirty minutes work-

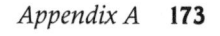

Start and end each putting session with short putts.

ing on their putting expertise before their round. After all, a good portion of their strokes will take place on the green.

Practice on off days becomes a division between stroke mechanics and drills, long putts and drills, short putts and drills, straight putts and drills, and breaking putts and drills. All should have visual dominance as a guidance tool attached to them.

"Practice green mentality" could include a schedule of 20 percent mechanical, 20 percent aim, 20 percent distance, 20 percent green reading and 20 percent routine.

Decide which areas of this book are going to be a focus, and set ways and means to practice them. Say you need to work on your moderate to long putts. You know you must start by walking off the distance of each and every one to make this a habit. You also know that you need to factor in pre-putt visualization to your routine, so you write down notes to that effect. After that, time could be spent on the stroke, incorporating tips that your pro gave you when he measured your visual positioning. Then it is short-putt time, when you want to work on aiming the logo. Then time could be spent on green reading. The important thing is to first know what you are looking for. Combine your knowledge of what you learned in this book with a green-reading lesson from your personal pro. Work to see what is there.

A Great Putting Drill

There is no substitute for practice. While you have a plethora of drills and techniques available to you in this book, putting drills are still a popular pastime on the putting green. A favorite putting drill encourages putting from increments of three feet, attempting to get the ball anywhere inside an area that would be from the hole to seventeen inches past the hole. Place tees in the ground at three, six, nine, twelve, fifteen, and so on.

Putt one ball from each tee. If the ball does not stop in the "square,"
you must start again from the first tee.

To start, putt one ball from the closest tee to the designated area, then move back to the next tee, and the next and so on. The only way you can gain the right to move back to the next tee is to stop your ball inside the designated area. If unsuccessful, you must go back to the first tee and start again.

This drill encourages you to compute the necessary speed to hit the ball seventeen inches past the hole. You can play this game with your buddies on the practice green, the winner being the one who advances the farthest from the starting tee.

The secrets to gaining the most out of this drill are:

1. Seeing the ball roll before stroking it. (By using visualization of the ball's speed or in-vision-ing before the putt, you are more inclined to make consistently well-paced putts from all distances.)
2. Putting only one ball. (This keeps you from falling into the tactile trap of only feeling the stroke.)

Thoughts on Bifocals, Ultraviolet Protection, Sunglasses, and Contact Lenses

Most golfers wearing bifocals would benefit from a specialty pair out on the course. See your eye doctor.

A regular bifocal could cause the ball to appear to jump for those who look through the bifocal when addressing the ball. This "parallax" is the result of the lens power focused for a much closer distance (than the ball). When the head moves even slightly, the ball can appear to move also. The player then anchors his head or restricts her stroke. The golfer may be able to adjust to this, with time, but why add to the complexity of the task? Those who aren't bothered by a bifocal may be sacrificing a specific

A regular bifocal can hinder your ability to make a full turn.

A bifocal only on the player's lens, that is opposite their lead foot when putting, allows for an interrupted look at the ball and down the line of the putt.

location of the ball or aren't looking at the ball with enough visual specifics.

Some golfers forsake glasses, because the bifocal interferes with their play. Good sight is helpful for better judgment of distances, locating your ball as it travels and lands, reading greens and reading the scorecard. For those who demand a single pair to do everything, my experience with the progressive ("no-line") has been very positive for most golfers.

If you do not wear a prescription necessary to see more clearly, then you are handicapping the visual even more. If one has to look hard or squint to see, this may lead to visual and physical fatigue. Refusal to wear glasses could risk visual "laziness" that can interfere with information processing such as green reading.

All golfers need to be aware that ultraviolet (UV) protection guards against possible cataracts and potential retinal

degenerations. UV, often referred to as blue light, represents the sun's shorter wavelengths (400–500 nanometers), and is the most damaging to the eye because of its higher energy radiation.

Blue light is not filtered out by the eye, so it reaches the retina and can also eventually affect night vision and light adaptation. Unlike the skin, the eyes do not develop a tolerance to repeated UV exposure.

You can obtain UV protection in a clear or colored coating. A tint also decreases squinting from the sun, which in turn relaxes the eyes. Relaxed eyes also relax the facial muscles and can keep the entire body's physiology more efficient.

The Bolle's Eagle Vision sunglasses are designed with the golfer in mind.

Wearing a colored lens outside is a matter of personal choice. If you do, we recommend choosing the least tint that keeps you from squinting yet allows the eye enough light to be comfortable while able to discern the subtleties of the greens to accurately read the breaks. Too dark a tint can cut out too much light and affect efficient functioning.

A good sunglass also reduces brightness and glare, protects against the wind's drying effect on the eyes and can help prevent unsightly and potentially damaging growths on the whites of the eye. Avoid cheap sunglasses that do not block UV rays. Possibly the best of the sunglasses to date is the "Eagle Vision" by Bolle. It appears to

have less lens distortion, and many golfers find them most comfortable to their eyes.

Contact lenses, soft or hard, can now correct almost any kind of visual acuity problem. If you are not wearing glasses because you can't get used to the distortion, ask your eye doctor about recent advances in contact lenses.

If contacts aren't in the cards, newer, high-index lenses and anti-reflective coatings may enhance your ability to wear glasses. Be careful when you have your eye exam. Especially those with astigmatism may pick a time after golf season to get their prescription filled. This gives you time to adjust to any change. By all means, communicate with your doctor if you have had problems adjusting to prescriptions before. This should signal the doctor to be careful not to overdo changes in astigmatism, especially axis changes. The doctor should also try to match the base curve of the lenses you are comfortable with now.

Types of Putters

Weight, height, hosel offset, blade, mallet—on and on go the choices you have available. Possibly one choice you may not have thought of, or may have arrived at but didn't know why, is which gives you the best visual for alignment. The ideal putter for those who align to a spot, or to a line, features a line that points toward the distance target.

Here are some other things to consider when selecting a putter:

1. Pick a putter with physical characteristics that are appealing to the *eyes*.
2. *See* whether the putter sits flat on the ground when you address the ball. It should.
3. *Look* at your hands when taking your address position—without a putter. If you like to keep your hands

A putter that is too flat for the player.　　　　*A putter that is too upright for the player.*

away from your body, you should choose a flat putter; close to your body, an upright model.

4. *Look* at your hands. If you like to keep them slightly ahead of the ball, use a putter with added loft; in line or slightly behind, one with less loft.

5. *Look* at the grip size; if it's thin and you have big hands, you may want to consider building it up. Furthermore, a thick grip prevents you from manipulating the putter with the hands. As always, ask your pro for assistance.

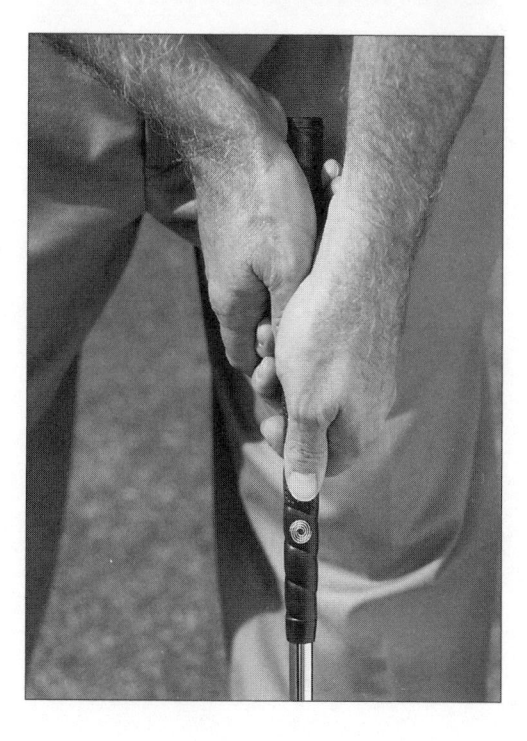

(top left)
Some players who are more motor-gifted prefer the handle to rest more in their fingers.

(top right)
I prefer most students to place the handle more in their palms.

(right)
The reverse, or left-hand-low grip position, helps you keep the left hand more in control during the stroke.

More Putting Tips (In Pictures)

(top left)
Too much forward lean of the shaft brought on by the hands too far forward at address.

(top right)
If the hands are too far back at address, the stroke will break down.

(left)
A proper position of the hands keeps the shaft more vertical.

The Closed Eye Technique

One technique that is common among golf's teachers is to ask the student to close their eyes and feel the stroke. They believe this shuts out visual noise and allows the player to just focus on the technique of the stroke. They have witnessed players putt better after using this technique in practice.

While this technique does allow for the player to focus on his stroke and, no doubt, some do putt better, the reason why often escapes the teacher. Vision is not always shut down when the eyes are closed. The only way to insure a shutdown is to also ask that they not visualize the stroke or the targets (the ball or the hole).

If the player needs emphasis on the smoothness of the stroke or taking it back straight, the closed eye method can be of some aid. Once again, focusing on a technique does have an advantage. It allows you to focus on the task of hitting the ball. But this emphasis on technique can become an avenue to undermine vision if overused.

I still prefer to let vision be the guiding force in the stroke by seeing the path from Target A to B, as well as to load the muscles through vision. But the most significant purpose of the closed eye technique, I believe, is in stimulating visualization of the ball and Target B. This higher level of visual performance skills should not be overlooked any time.

Self-assess Your Putting

The quality of your putting expertise becomes your ability to eliminate as many visual anomalies as possible and to plug in all of the factors on each and every putt.

DR. CRAIG L. FARNSWORTH
From a putting workshop at the 1993 Colorado PGA
Golf Academy

When playing your next round, use the "scorecard" below to record your putts. Place each putt *(putt them all)* in a category. For example, if the putt hit the hole in the center and was going the correct speed, place a check under the "Exact" column. If it hit the hole dead center but was too hard, place it under the "Long" category.

EXACT	SHORT	LONG	LEFT	RIGHT	SHORT/ RIGHT	SHORT/ LEFT	LONG/ RIGHT	LONG/ LEFT

Glossary of Terms

Aiming Accuracy:

The ability to correctly interpret the X-axis projection of an object in space. If incorrect, the object appears to the left or right of actual. This misperception of reality can be caused by a peripheral vision restriction, an eye-teaming problem and/or a problem with the neck-back muscles.

Alignment:

The ability to reference the body's and club's position to an object of regard (the hole or a target spot on the green). It is also dependent on the individual's ability to appreciate his or her body awareness and awareness of the clubface when "square" to the target. Highly dependent on X-axis accuracy of perception.

Depth Perception:

The eyes' ability to judge distances in relation to other distances.

Direction:

In putting, it is the path chosen for the ball. It relates to alignment of the clubface to the target. It's accuracy is highly visually related.

Directional Visualization Accuracy:

The ability of the eyes to (accurately) reference the target in space (past arm's length). This depends upon the eye muscles' ability to point to (locate) the object, and the peripheral retina's ability to align the eyes to the target.

Dominant Eye:

The eye that is the most accurate at referencing where the object is in relation to the individual. Also referred to as the "aiming eye." Established involuntarily in the early years of development.

Fine-tune:

Narrowing the focus of the eye to as small a spot as possible. This entails avoiding peripheral areas that may be distracting, or that will widen the area of regard and potentially result in a mis-hit.

Future Time Zone:

A point in time that has not yet occurred or is about to occur, including pre-round rehearsal.

Goal:

The desired outcome of a performance (e.g., to make the putt). A future occurrence that is a positive outcome from the task facing the individual.

Information Processing:

The purpose of information processing is to originate a stimulus, or attend to one, for an appropriate motor response, in order to come to terms with environmental conditions effectively.

In-vision-ing:

A term coined by the author referring to the ability of the eyes' ocular muscles to self-direct and be a stimulus that will impart, to the rest of the body, the speed, or pace, of the putt that is about to be undertaken. This term was coined because of the lack of accurate visualization skills of the majority of athletes observed by the author.

Localization:

The ability of the individual to perceive the distance and direction of an object in space. This skill is based on several factors, including the peripheral retina and the neck and ocular muscles. A combination of the accuracy of perception of the X and Y and Z axes.

Mental:

Referencing the brain and controlling its functioning. The mind is shown to be controlled best through visual dominance.

Motor Driving the Motor:

A phrase used by the author to connote the level of learning where the muscles are directing themselves. This applies most when one is learning a new technique, or when the visual is unable to impart information correctly or accurately.

Ocular Muscles:

The six muscles of each eye that are involved in tracking a moving object or fixating on a stationary object.

Past Time Zone:

Referencing that which happened previously. Those who are tactile processors are more prone to "live in the past," and thus have to work harder at staying in the present.

Present Time Zone:

That which is happening at the moment (separate from past or future references). The basis for all successful performance, and the "here and now" of information processing. Highly dependent on the visual system.

See-do:

"Letting it happen" as opposed to thinking too much.

Selective Attention:

The choosing of a sensory system to be the primary information-processing stimulus for the task.

Self-direction:

The skill or ability to be in control of the situation, primarily by using visualization to direct the action, instead of reacting to a stimulus. Requires the individual to prepare and plan for the action to follow.

Soft Focus:

When the individual is observing a large field of view by utilizing the peripheral retina.

Spatial Visualization Accuracy:

The ability to (accurately) project the location of an object in space as to its distance in relation to the individual.

Target A:

The ball.

Target B:

The (final) point on the green that is now the projected place to direct the eyes toward the actual hole. This point is based on several factors, including grain, slope and individual characteristics. This point combines the aim point and the stimulus for the energy for the stroke.

Task:

The job the individual is faced with at that moment. Is also referenced as the "here and now," or the Present Time Zone, where the person is focused away from future goals or past situations.

Tension Control:

The ability of the individual to maintain sufficient energy of the muscles for the motor action to follow.

Time:

One of the two cornerstones of performance. Relates to the distance between two points. In putting, it becomes the distance from the ball to the target, the green characteristics and the pace necessary to get the ball to the hole.

Visual Alignment:

The ability of the eyes to accurately "team" or point to/at an object. Inaccurate teaming can cause one or both to perceive objects as closer or farther away, or right or left of their actual location.

Visual Concentration:

Exercising control of the visual system.

Visual Dominance:

Placing the visual sensory system as the primary system for processing information.

Visual Driving the Motor:

Utilizing the visual sensory system to program or direct the muscles to act in a defined manner. Allowing the eyes to direct the body. Seeing the action that is to take place, and letting the muscles react to the visual stimulus.

Visual Guidance:

Using the eyes, and often the eye muscles, to accurately align the body and the club to a specific point in space.

Visualization:

The regeneration of a previously seen stimulus. A self-directed skill that Webster's dictionary defines as "to form a mental image or vision of."

Visual Perspective:

The individual's perception of reality.

Visual Positioning:

Pertains to the accurate relationship of the eyes to the ball, the ball to the feet and the body in relation to the target.

X-axis:

The spatial perception of direction, relating to alignment to the target, or misalignment to the left or right of actual.

Yips:

A term used to connote a muscle spasm in the fingers or hands during the putting stroke. This is often called a "neurological quirk," but its foundation comes from lack of a positive image of the outcome.

Y-axis:

The spatial perception that relates to the hole being above or below the plane of the ball.

Z-axis:

The spatial perception that relates to the actual distance from the ball to the hole.

Index

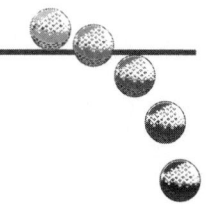

Note: Page numbers with an *f* indicate figures.

15% off

any SEE schools or products with this gift certificate

"Dr. Farnswor

was instrumen

in my winni

the 1996 Master

NICK FALL

MASTERING THE GAME

~at the Jim McLean Golf School at the beautiful PGA West Resort. We offer the most comprehensive long game and short game schools in the world. You will be instructed by the top coaches and instructors in the country. For all levels of play we offer:

One Day See It & Sink It School
Two Day Scoring School
Three Day Short Game School
Five Day Elite School

S E E   I T   &   S I N K   I T

Other SEE, Inc. products guaranteed to help you improve...

SEE IT & SINK IT TRAINING SYSTEM:

Putting must become a valuable part of your golf arsenal in order to maximize your scoring potential. During a round, a player will average 8 to 12 putts from three feet to fifteen feet, resulting in a difference from a 68 to a 76, or an 89 compared to a 100. The SEE IT & SINK IT TRAINING SYSTEM FOR PUTTING is the first golf training product scientifically proven to dramatically improve your game. The system improves the four keys towards putting excellence.

1. Accurate alignment
2 Mastering green reading
3. Target distance
4. Speed and tempo

The SEE IT & SINK IT TRAINING SYSTEM includes:

1. THE SCORING LINE
2. SURE PUTT™
3. SEE IT & SINK IT INSTRUCTIONAL VIDEO
4. RHYTHMIC STROKE GUIDE
5. REFERENCE CARD

Masterir

Putting an

Concentratio

Schools ar

Produc

SEE IT & SINK IT

THE INNER WORKINGS OF GOLF TRAINING VIDEO™~

All golfers, including tour pros, have shortcomings in their game which can stand improvement. In over 15 years of training recreational and professional golfers, as well as other athletes, Dr. Craig Farnsworth shows you why the eyes have it in golf. Through his unique visual guidance drills and techniques, you will better master your scoring potential. This video emphasizes the short game and particularly putting to enhance even your concentration skills. Dr. Farnsworth will show you why some of your problems are perceptual in nature and offer you easily applied techniques to overcome areas that are stalling your improvement. The "Inner Workings Golf Training Video™" helps golfers of any age, gender and skill level instantly improve. You will enjoy Dr. Farnsworth's stories concerning his work with some of the players listed below.

Dr. Farnsworth has worked with the following professional golfers:
Nick Faldo, Jesper Parnevik, Tom Kite, Bobby Wadkins, Ted Purdy,
Jay Sigel, Brad Faxon, Tom Purtzer, Grant Waite, Steve Elkington,
Andrew Magee, Jill McGill, Dale Douglas, Mark Wiebe, Rocco Mediate,
Bernhard Langer, Trevor Dodds, John Mahaffey, Isao Aoki,
Peter Jacobsen, Keith Fergus, Billy Andrade, Jane Geddes, Hal Sutton,
Peter Kostis, Don Bies

For brochures, school bookings and product ordering, or for more information please contact us at:

"You will learn drills that will last you for a lifetime of golfing pleasure."

DR. FARNSWORTH

JIM MCLEAN
GOLF SCHOOL
PGA WEST

SPORTS EYE ENHANCEMENTS
1999 BROADWAY ▪ SUITE 2400 ▪ DENVER, COLORADO 80202
VOICE (303) 292-9200 ▪ FAX (303) 299-9565
WWW.EYEMINDBODY.COM

W9-BOB-395